HARRY POTTER
AND
HARRYPOTTER

The author of this book has pledged (without a Torah oath) to donate 10% of all of his proceeds from sales of this book to schools in Israel that serve the educational needs of children of English-speaking families.

E-mail: author@harrypottertorah.com
Web site: http://www.harrypottertorah.com

DEDICATION

This book is dedicated to my children
who introduced me to Harry Potter
and put up with how much I enjoyed it.

May things they enjoy
find connections to Torah

and may Torah always be
something they enjoy.

Abraham held an historic summit with the spiritual elder of the time Malki-Tzedek. Abraham wanted to learn more about how to reach the masses and teach them about G-d. We don't have record of their conversation, but we do know that Malki-Tzedek brought out some bread and he brought out some wine. The message: bread is best when it's fresh – the older it gets the less usable. Wine is not wine until it ages – the older the better.

Malki-Tzedek taught Abraham the secret of the bread and the wine. When teaching people about G-d, the main course must be the old and beautiful traditions that make up the essence of Torah. Give them wine. But always remember, Malki-Tzedek taught, to serve fresh bread. We are all starving for the traditions of old, but at the same time we yearn for that new, refreshing and invigorating bread.

In this very creative edition Dov Krulwich serves us wine and he serves us bread. The successful educator is he or she that can teach the wisdom of the generations in the language of the times. Dov fills this role with brilliance as he takes one of the world's most contemporary interests and masterfully uses it to teach Torah. A contribution that utilizes the vogue yet maintains its integrity is truly a cause for celebration. I await more.

Rabbi Yaacov Haber

13 Kupperman Lane Monsey NY 10952
212.561.5045   info@torahlab.org
www.torahlab.org

4

Table of contents

Preface 7
Introduction 9
In the Beginning There Were Magic Words 17
Talking Snakes and Human Souls 26
Day of Rest, Day of Magic 33
Noah's Care of Magical Creatures 40
Owl post, Raven post, and dove post 45
Ghosts and curtains 50
Mudbloods, Moabites, and Moshiach 60
Whomping Willows & Monotheistic Maples 69
Everyday Magic, Everyday Miracles 75
Nicolas Flamel and the Children of Ketura 84
When One Rises, the Other Will Fall 91
Destiny and Decisions 96
Magic Wands 101
Go to the Hippogriff, thy Sluggard 113
Creating Bodies 118
Rights of Magical Creatures 129
Dreams: Divination or Digestion? 135
Everything Happens for a Reason 143
We are as Strong as we are United 148
Magic Shows: Kosher Fun or Idolatry? 161
Magical Protection 168
Epilogue 176
Sources quoted 178
Index of Citations 191
Subject index 197

Preface

Some people will feel ill at ease about this book, with a vague fear that a book connecting Torah concepts to Harry Potter is inappropriate, that it risks diminishing the honor of Torah and reducing it to the level of pop fiction, G-d forbid.

I share this concern. And I answer with the following three points:

First, this is not a book about Harry Potter, it is a book of Torah-true Jewish insights that I have related to ideas raised in Harry Potter. Every chapter in this book stands on its own as an interesting idea from traditional Jewish thought, with footnotes to sources in the Talmud and the Midrash, Jewish Law, and the Chassidic and Mussar schools. It is the selection of the ideas, and the way in which they are introduced and explained, that relate them to Harry Potter, but every concept is pure Torah.

Second, many people unfortunately think that Torah has nothing to say about their areas of interest. And yet, our sages tell us that we should "study it and study it (Torah), because everything is in it"[1]. Nothing is "outside" of Torah, even technology and business, even, I daresay, the ideas raised by the magical (and fictional) world of Harry Potter. I hope that this book will show the richness of Torah and its ability to relate to all aspects of life and all areas of interest.

---

[1] Pirkei Avot 5:25

Third, very simply, there is nothing wrong with Judaism and Torah being fun. Jewish children traditionally start their first day of learning to read Hebrew by licking honey off letters in a book and identifying the letter. Passover Seders traditionally include candies and snacks to keep kids interested and involved. Should Torah be any less fun for teens and adults?

Whether or not these points answer the concern, and whether this book achieves these aims, is up to The One True Judge, Who separates between the Holy and the profane, and Who commanded us to study and adhere to His Torah with happiness and a joyous heart[2].

---

[2] Deut 28:47

Introduction

The ideas presented in this book were developed week by week over a four year period, and discussed at the Shabbos and YomTov table with family, friends, and guests. Some received them passionately, some cynically, some curiously, but everyone enjoyed them.

I wrote this book knowing that different people will pick it up with different expectations about what it contains, and most would be wrong. Many will expect it to be a book for children; in fact it is aimed at young adults or teenagers. Many will expect it to reflect a liberal or new age approach to Jewish belief and practice; in fact it reflects a traditional outlook and is based on traditional sources throughout.

Traditional Jewish sources discussing owl post, magic wands, magical travel, and ghosts? Yes!

Most of the chapters in this book follow a pattern common in traditional Jewish writings. First, a general idea or question is presented from the Harry Potter series, raising the question of what the Torah has to say on the subject. Then, a quote is given from the Torah, Talmud, or other classic Jewish source, which most often raises additional questions of its own. These questions are then answered with references to commentaries and other sources, and the concepts presented in the answer then answer the original "Harry Potter question" raised at the beginning.

The chapters are loosely organized around the Torah portions of the book of Genesis (Bereisheet in Hebrew, commonly Bereishis). The chapters can, however, be read in any order.

The Jewish sources that are quoted throughout the book span the broad spectrum of Jewish scholarship. Every chapter includes quotes from the Torah itself, and most from the Talmud or Midrash. Some chapters are focused on Jewish practice, and quote heavily from the Shulchan Aruch and other, more contemporary, books of Jewish Law (Halacha). Some are more mystical, and quote from Kabbalistic or Chassidic writings. Some are focused on ethics and morality, based on the writings of the Mussar (ethical) school. Many chapters combine all of the above.

Torah and Talmud, Midrash, Kabbalah and Halacha

A full explanation of various Jewish writings is not the point of this book, and the book is written to be enjoyed by people with any amount of Jewish education (or none). But some readers might want an understanding of a little bit of the traditional perspectives that the book takes for granted. If you do not, feel free to skip this section.

The traditional Jewish perspective is that the Jewish people received the Torah, the "Five Books of Moses," directly from G-d on Mount Sinai and in the Sinai desert. This did not only include the Ten Commandments; it also included the Torah itself. G-d also explained the Torah to Moses, and Moses then spent 40 years asking G-d questions and receiving G-d's elaboration and explanation of exactly what He meant by things He said in the Torah. In this way, both the Torah and its explanation are of Divine origin. The Torah itself was not meant to be taken literally, rather to be understood with G-d's explanation to Moses. This explanation was passed down verbally, from parent to child and from teacher to student, called "the Oral Torah."

By the time of the Second Temple, however, the communication from teacher to student began to break down. At that point the sages began to put the Oral Torah in writing, first in the Mishna and then in the Gemorah, together called the Talmud. Each are collections of opinions of different sages on a wide variety of subjects, all of which are considered to be Torah-true principles, but for which it may not be clear how they all fit together and when each principle applies.

In addition to writing down Jewish practice, the sages wanted to record Torah perspectives on ethics and general behavior. Rather than describing these directly, they taught them in story form, called the Midrash (plural being "midrashim") and Aggadah. Some midrashim describe things that actually happened, some may not (see below), but all reflect Divine ethical and moral lessons.

Most subsequent Jewish writing, until the modern day, tends to focus either on Jewish Law (halacha), or Ethics and morality, or mysticism (kabbalah). The most scholarly of these writings are in the area of Halacha, Jewish law. These build heavily on each other through the generations, applying Torah principles to new situations that arise, and resolving what to do when two contradictory principles apply in a given real-world situation.

Lastly, the Oral Torah was understood by the sages also to include mystical teachings, explaining how the physical world fits into the spiritual realms. These teachings explain concepts from the prophets, and teach other mystical ideas that G-d revealed. The primary book of Kabbalah is the Zohar, written around the time of the Mishna, but there are many other texts as well, such as Sefer Yetzira (the Book of Creation) and Sefer HaBahir (Book of Illumination).

It is important to keep in mind that all categories of Torah are meant to fit together into a cohesive whole. Scholarship has a tendency to specialize, but Torah is fundamentally a single unit.

Are Midrashim "true?"

When people read hard-to-believe Midrashic stories, whether supernatural, seemingly primitive, or just far-fetched, there is a tendency to react in one of two ways. Some people feel a religious imperative to believe in the literal truth of the Midrash. Others are driven to dismiss it totally, to discard any story that clashes with common sense as "just a story."

A middle-ground traditional approach, taken by this book, is not to worry about the literal truth of Midrash, but attempt rather to learn the moral or behavioral lessons that the sages were trying to teach through the story. The sages wrote Midrashim to teach something, and we can learn from them regardless of whether we accept them as literal truth.

As Rabbi Moshe Chayim Lutzatto wrote: "Many fundamental ideas are hinted to by our Sages in Midrashim discussing scientific or material things, which make use of teachings that were taught in those times by their wise men and scientists. However, the central point of these Midrashim is not the scientific issue, but rather the principle or secret to which they hinted. Therefore, do not consider the truth of the hinted principle on the basis on the analogy in which it is "clothed," because their intent was to convey the principle inside the "clothing" of an analogy that was accepted by the wise men of that era. They could also have conveyed the principle in other ways, appropriate for other generations."[3]

Based on this approach, when we present Midrashim such as Naftali's supernatural running abilities (end of the chapter on Magic Shows) or the Phoenix's immortality (chapter on the Magical Phoenix), we will try to learn and apply the lessons that our sages were teaching, regardless of the literal truth of the Midrash.

But is it really Judaism?

Many people will be surprised at the broad range of ideas presented as "Jewish" in this book, particularly the more esoteric subjects like ghosts and magic wands. This is one reason that citations

---

[3] Al Ha'agados, path 3; see also Rambam's introduction to The Guide to the Perplexed and Maharasha's introduction to his Talmud commentary.

have been provided throughout, connecting the chapters here to the traditional Jewish sources on which they are based.

Does a "good Jew" have to believe in the more offbeat concepts presented here? Strictly speaking, the answer is no; any Jew who lives a life of Jewish practice, adhering to the commandments and believing in the core Jewish beliefs, is certainly fulfilling what G-d asks of a Jew. Rambam's thirteen principles of faith, alluded to in his writings and listed in many prayer books (and the basis of the "Yigdal" prayer), list thirteen core beliefs of Judaism, and esoteric concepts are not among them.

I hope, however, that skeptics will at least think about the following: Even if you maintain your healthy skepticism, do you really want to close off all possibility of offbeat things really existing in the world? Is there not a certain comfort and intrigue in the idea that there might be more to the world than we see, that G-d created the supernatural along with the natural?

Final few things

Anyone writing Jewish books in English is faced with the question of how to translate and/or transliterate Hebrew words and verses into English. My personal preference is to transliterate Hebrew phrases and names, to keep the distinctions and flavor of the original Hebrew. I have deferred, however, to the common practice of using common English (Moses instead of Moshe, Hebron instead of Chevron), which will be more familiar to most readers. I have also used Modern Hebrew transliterations in place of traditional transliterations for the same reason.

All verses and other Hebrew sources have been re-translated into English during the writing of this book, often taking into account the commentary or perspective that is being discussed. Hebrew transliterations are sometimes given as well, especially in cases where the Hebrew words themselves are significant.

Most of all, the book has been written to be fun to read and interesting to think about.

Acknowledgements

My biggest thanks go to the family, friends, and guests that served as the sounding board for these ideas at Shabbos and YomTov meals over the years, first in Har Nof, Jerusalem, and later in Beit Shemesh. This book would not have been possible without your interest and enthusiasm.

Huge thanks go to everyone who reviewed drafts of the book and helped me turn it from a bunch of words into (I hope) a clear and cohesive book. Particular thanks go to my first readers, my parents, Lewis and Maxine Krulwich; my mother's comments in particular made the first complete draft readable. I am grateful to Rav Yaacov Haber and Rav Avishai David, who devoted more of their time than I expected to reading drafts and giving me their comments. I am also grateful to Barbara Brown, David Gerwin, Paulette Posner, and some anonymous readers for their comments and suggestions. After all this great help, any mistakes or bad writing are entirely my own fault.

The full first draft of this book was written completely on my pocket "smartphone" computer, likely the first Torah book that can make such a claim. Most of the writing happened on the bus between Beit Shemesh and Jerusalem. For this I thank Nokia and Egged. Much of the rest was written in Shuls and Batei Midrash, notably Beis Midrash Heichal Avraham, Beit Midrash Torani Leumi, Beit Knesset Feigenson, and Kahal Chassidim Anshei Yerushalayim, all in Beit Shemesh, and I thank them for use of their books and space.

At the end of our prayers, three times a day, we ask G-d to "give us our portion in [His] Torah," indicating that every Jew has a unique portion of G-d's Torah that he or she can uniquely excel in learning or carrying out. This book may be proof of how unique such portions may be; for this, and everything else, I thank Him.

Dov (Bruce) Krulwich
Beit Shemesh, Israel
December, 2006
Kislev, 5767

In the Beginning There Were Magic Words

Bereisheet #1

In Harry Potter's world we know that most magic requires that the wizard say an incantation out loud and clearly, as Harry and his classmates are taught in the first book:

> *"Now, don't forget..." squeaked Professor Flitwick, "... saying the magic words properly is very important... never forget Wizard Baruffio, who said 's' instead of 'f' and found himself on the floor with a buffalo on his chest." (Sorcerer's Stone, chapter 10)*

Later, in Half Blood Prince, Harry and his friends learn about doing magic without speaking, which is possible but is much harder:

> *"... You are, I believe, complete novices in the use of non-verbal spells.*
> *...*
> *"Not all wizards can do this, of course; it is a question of concentration and mind power...." (Half Blood Prince, chapter 9)*

Why should speech matter so much in performing magic?

Jewish tradition tells us that speaking out loud is very important in Jewish practice as well. The Jewish activity that is similar to Harry Potter's magic is prayer, in which we ask G-d to supernaturally change the world in ways that we want. Prayer, like magical incantations in the world of Harry Potter, should ideally be spoken out loud. Another activity in which we'll see the importance of speaking out loud is Torah study, in which we try to learn supernatural lessons and bring them into our lives.

It must be remembered that prayer and Torah study are not themselves magic. Saying a prayer is not the same thing as saying a magical incantation. Rather, our prayers are communication with G-d, and our Torah study is our trying to learn G-d's lessons for life. They're only being discussed here as analogies for incantations, in that they are a primary way that we can interact with the supernatural.

The Mishna says the following in the discussion of saying the Shma prayer each day:

"If someone says Shma, but not loud enough to be heard in his own ear, he has still fulfilled his obligation. Rav Yossi says he has not."[4]

The Talmud explains that Rav Yossi bases his opinion on the word "Shma," which means "hear," while the rest of the sages disagreed and said that it is not obligatory to be able to hear yourself saying Shma. This principle, that it is important to say Shma out loud but that it is minimally sufficient not to, is codified as Jewish Law in the Shulchan Aruch:

---

[4] Brachot 15a

"Everyone must say Shma loud enough to hear his words in his own ear, but if someone said Shma and couldn't hear his words in his own ear he is considered to have fulfilled his obligation, as long as he at least made some amount of sound"[5].

The Talmud continues to discuss speaking out loud for other prayers:

"The previous discussion was about saying Shma, but for other commandments, all agree that someone who says them without hearing his words has fulfilled his obligation."[6]

This is explained and cited as practical Jewish law in the Shulchan Aruch:

"Blessing after meals can be said in any language, and must be said so that the person can hear his own words, but if the person couldn't hear his own words, he has fulfilled his obligation, as long as he made some sound."[7]

Other Halacha sources[8] say the same thing about other blessings.

We see from these sources that Jewish tradition views prayer remarkably similarly to how Harry Potter discusses magical incantations. With concentration, when necessary, prayer can be accomplished without speaking out loud, but to be done properly, prayers must be spoken.

---

[5] Shulchan Aruch Orech Chayim 62:3
[6] Brachot 15b
[7] Shulchan Aruch Orech Chayim 185:1-2
[8] Shulchan Aruch Orech Chayim 206:3, Rambam Hilchos Brachot chapter 1

As an aside, the concept of praying out loud does not necessitate praying so loudly that others can hear you. Many sources actually discourage this[9] based on the story of the prayer of Chana, the mother of Samuel the Prophet, which describes her prayer as quiet[10]. Other sources give advantages to loud prayer. Our point here is that prayers cannot be fully silent, and need to be given form by making at least some sound.

The same is true of how we study Torah. Many people have observed that while secular libraries are quiet places, Jewish study halls tend to be loud and active. One reason is the following statement by the Shulchan Aruch, on the subject of the Blessing that should be said in the morning before studying any Torah, called Birkat HaTorah:

"Someone who only thinks Torah thoughts in his head does not need to say Birkat HaTorah first"[11]. The Mishna Berurah elaborates: "This is because thinking is not like speech. Therefore, it is important for people who study from books to at least say some Torah out loud (in order to fulfill their Mitzvah to study Torah)."[12]

The Shulchan Aruch is saying that unspoken Torah study does not fully "count" as Torah study, to the degree that the blessing said before studying

---

[9] Mishna Berurah 101:6; Zohar VaYigash 209b, quoted in Chok LeYisrael Maasei for Wednesday

[10] Samuel 1:1:13

[11] Shulchan Aruch Orech Chayim 47:4

[12] Mishna Berurah 47:5

Torah does not need to be said before unspoken Torah thinking.[13]

We see clearly from this that Jewish sources want us to speak out loud, when possible, so that our Prayers and Torah study will leave our heads and enter the world.

Commentaries explain the essence of speech as taking our thoughts, which are unexpressed, and giving them expression. Thoughts that are purely in our heads have no tangible form, but thoughts that have been expressed can move from the thinker out into the world, where they can have an influence, spiritual or practical. Speaking is literally a creative act, with as much tangible effect on the world as physical actions[14]. Moreover, human distinctiveness and vitality comes from our ability to speak, so only by speaking out loud can our thoughts be connected to our vitality[15].

Amazingly, the Torah says that G-d Himself carried out creation of the world, the unique "magical" creation of something from nothing, through speech. In the creation chapter, as every part of the world is created, G-d first speaks about the thing to be created, and then the thing is created:

---

[13] Note that the Vilna Gaon disagrees with the Shulchan Aruch, and rules that thoughts are as powerful as speech, and that unspoken Torah requires that the blessing be said first. Correspondingly, he rules that it is prohibited to even think about Torah when in the bathroom, while the Mishna Berurah says that this is permitted (although not advisable) because thought is not as significant as speech. (Biyur Halacha on 47:4)

[14] Nefesh HaChayim sec 1 chapter 13

[15] Maharal, Netiv HaTorah, chapter 4; Nefesh HaChayim sec 2 chapter 13

"G-d said 'let there be light' and there was light."[16]

"G-d said 'Let there be a sky within the water."[17]

In Pirkei Avot,[18] the Ethics of the Fathers, the sages say that "the world was created with ten acts of speech." This speech wasn't the Torah's "literary license," and it wasn't incidental to creation, it was part of the essential process of creation, the method by which G-d created the world from nothingness. This is why the morning prayer services start with the sentence "Blessed is He who spoke and brought the world into being."[19]

The Talmud goes so far as to suggest that when G-d rested on the seventh day of creation, He rested from speech, since He carried out his creation through speech, and that on the Sabbath we should refrain from talking![20] But the Talmud concludes that since the Torah later commands us to observe the Sabbath by refraining from constructive work, that speech in general is of course permitted.[21]

The ten speech acts are:

1. In the beginning G-d created the heavens and the earth[22]

---

[16] Gen 1:3

[17] Gen 1:6

[18] Mishna 5:1

[19] In Hebrew: Baruch She'amar

[20] Talmud Yerushalmi Shabbos 15:3 (78a), and Shirei Korban commentary there

[21] Tosfos commentary on Shabbos 113b; see also Midrash Vayikra Raba 34:16

[22] Gen 1:1 (based on the Talmudic discussion in Megila 21b and Rosh HaShana 32a)

2. "Let there be light"[23]

3. "Let there be a sky within the water"[24]

4. "Let the water beneath the sky be gathered"[25]

5. "Let the earth sprout vegetation"[26]

6. "Let there be luminaries in the sky"[27]

7. "Let the water fill with creatures, and birds fly"[28]

8. "Let the earth bring forth animals"[29]

9. "Let us make man"[30]

10. "It is not good for Man to be alone, I will make him a partner corresponding to him"[31],[32]

The point of the Mishna is that G-d's speech during the Torah's account of creation wasn't incidental, it was part of the process of creation. Even for G-d Himself, the act of changing nature, of

---

[23] Gen 1:3
[24] Gen 1:6
[25] Gen 1:9
[26] Gen 1:11
[27] Gen 1:14
[28] Gen 1:20
[29] Gen 1:24
[30] Gen 1:26
[31] Gen 2:18
[32] Some say the 10th speech act is ."Behold, I have given you every plant... and every tree...." (Gen 1:29), and some include "the spirit of G-d moved on the surface of the water" (Gen 1:2), see Midrash Bereisheet Raba 17:1 for discussion of the various opinions.

truly creating or changing the world, required speech.

The connection of speech to magic is even alluded to in some magical incantations themselves. The "magic words" we have all heard magicians use, Abra Kedabra, is not found anywhere in the Harry Potter series, but the worst of the three unforgivable curses, the killing curse, sounds remarkably similar: Avada Kedavra. Why do these two spells sound so alike, and why do they sound so different from the other incantations in the Harry Potter books, most of which end in "-us" or "-um" or "-io"?

The answer may lie in the fact that these two incantations have their roots in the Hebrew language (popularized through Aramaic by the Arabian Knights), while all the others are from Latin. This is clear from lists put together by Harry Potter fans[33] which give Latin roots for every spell in the books, with Avada Kedavra the only one with an Aramaic root.

"Abra" in Hebrew means "I will create," from the same root as the word "bara" in the first line in the Torah, "Bereisheet Bara," in the beginning G-d created. "K'adabra" means "as I will speak," from the Hebrew word "diber," to speak. So "abra kedabra" means, in Hebrew, "I will create as I will speak," an appropriate description of most magic.

Avada means "I will destroy." We see this in the Book of Esther, when Haman tries "to wipe out, kill and destroy ("le'hashmid, le'harog u'le'abed") all the

---

[33] Several such lists of spells from the Harry Potter series can be found on the Internet.

Jews." The Hebrew "le'abed" is from the same root as "avada," since the Hebrew letters for "b" and "v" are the same (with or without a dot in the middle). We also see this word in the daily "tachanun" prayer, where we beg G-d "al yo'vad Yisrael," do not let the Jewish people be destroyed, where the prefix "yo" is the grammatical conjugation for third person future tense. "Kedavra" means the same as "kedabra," "as I will speak," with the b and v again interchangeable in Hebrew.

So the killing curse in Harry Potter, "avada kedavra," the one incantation in Harry Potter that does not sound Latin, means in Hebrew "I will destroy as I speak," a fitting translation. Both of these relate magic directly to the act of saying incantations out loud.

In the world of Harry Potter, we do see that some magic can be performed without speech, but only with "concentration and mind power." In Torah thought, too, we have seen that prayer and Torah study can accomplish their goals to some extent even when not spoken out loud. But if we really want our words to have their effect, we should try to pray and study Torah out loud.

We may not achieve "abra kedabra," and we may not create a world, but we may find that our words of prayer and Torah study can truly have a magical effect.

Talking Snakes and Human Souls

Bereisheet #2

The Harry Potter books are full of talking animals. From the very start of the first book we see snakes talking, and magical creatures like house elves and centaurs have a lot to say throughout the series:

> *"The great snake was uncoiling itself rapidly, slithering out onto the floor. People throughout the reptile house screamed and started running for the exits. As the snake slid swiftly past him, Harry could have sworn a low, hissing voice said 'Brazil, here I come ... Thanksss, amigo.' "(The Sorcerer's Stone, chapter 2)*

And later, when Harry meets Dobby the House Elf:

> *"Harry managed not to shout out, but it was a close thing. The little creature on the bed had large, bat-like ears and bulging green eyes.... 'Harry Potter!' said the creature in a high-pitched voice... 'So long has Dobby wanted to meet you, sir....' " (Chamber of Secrets, chapter 2)*

All these talking animals raise an obvious question: What does the Torah say about talking animals?

When the Torah describes the creation of human beings, G-d gives us "a living soul" that is unique to mankind among all created life[34]. The explanatory translation of Onkolus, written around the year 90 CE, explains "living soul" as "soul that can speak." This reflects the idea that the power of speech comes from the human soul, and that only human beings are capable of truly thoughtful speech. Animals can communicate, but truly thoughtful speech is unique to humans.

But this raises a harder question: If the Torah attributes the power of speech only to humans, how do Biblical stories include speaking animals?

The first talking animal in the Torah is the snake in the Garden of Eden[35]. How did the snake talk to Eve if it didn't have a human soul?

Commentaries suggest that the snake may not have spoken like a person did, but rather in snake language, which Eve understood[36], making her (in Harry Potter terminology) the first parselmouth. But this only addresses the language spoken, and doesn't answer how the snake could have spoken at all.

There are two common explanations of how the snake spoke without having a human soul. The first is that the snake was originally created to be a servant of mankind, and was given a partial ability to

---

[34] Gen 2:7
[35] Gen chapter 3
[36] Ibn Ezra on Gen 3:1

speak. In the words of the Maharasha's commentary on the Talmud[37]:

"The entire creation was made for the use of mankind, but the snake was originally created to be the choice servant, in the middle between humans and other animals. That is why we find in it (the snake) the power of speech, and why it was 'the most cunning of all the animals'[38]."

After the snake enticed Eve to eat from the tree of knowledge, it was punished by G-d by having its nature changed. Rather than serve mankind, it would spend its life crawling on the ground, and would be both feared and hurt by people.

As a second explanation of the snake's speech, the Seforno commentary interprets the snake's role in the story completely allegorically. In the Seforno's words:

"The snake... is the evil inclination.... The Torah refers to concepts using familiar words, such as referring to a king as a lion... In this way the evil inclination which tempts people is called 'snake' for it is similar to a snake, which has limited value but great ability to damage, though small in appearance."[39]

According to the Seforno's commentary, the snake is allegorical for mankind's "evil inclination" ("yetzer ha'rah" in Hebrew), similar to the "id" in Freudian psychology, which drives people to act according to desires rather than what they know rationally to be

---

[37] Sanhedrin 59b
[38] Gen 3:1
[39] Seforno on Gen 3:1

best. In the Seforno's view, Eve wasn't a victim of an external force, rather of the temptations felt by her own psyche, which the Torah describes allegorically as a snake.

Other commentaries elaborate on this "allegorical snake" in a more comprehensive view of the whole story of Adam and Eve in the Garden of Eden. When Adam and Eve were first created, they were given a single command by G-d: do not eat from the tree of knowledge of good and bad. At this stage of creation, in the Garden of Eden, they had the ability to distinguish right from wrong, but did not have the feelings of good and bad that we have today, and did not have the emotional drive to do things that were wrong. This emotional drive to do wrong things was external to them, represented by the snake. After eating from the tree of knowledge of good and bad, human beings were infused with an internal evil inclination that drove them to act not according to right and wrong but according to what felt good and bad.

Whether we understand these explanations in an allegorical or literal sense, we've seen that all commentaries explain the snake as an anomaly. The general principle is that animals cannot speak because they lack a human soul, and the snake of the creation story is an exception to that rule, either created for a specific purpose, or discussed by the Torah allegorically to teach us a particular point.

What about other talking animals in the Torah? In the Torah portion of Balak we see the story of Bilam's donkey:

"G-d was angry that he (Bilam) was going, and an angel of G-d stood on the path to oppose him.... When the donkey saw G-d's angel standing on the road with a sword in his hand, the donkey went off the road into the field. Bilam hit the donkey to get it back to the road.

"G-d's angel then stood in a narrow path between vineyards, with a fence on both sides. When the donkey saw G-d's angel, it edged over to the side, crushing Bilam's leg against the fence. He beat it even more.

"G-d's angel continued ahead and stood in a narrow place where there was no room on either side. When the donkey saw G-d's angel, it lay down. Bilam got even angrier, and hit it with a stick.

"G-d then opened the mouth of the donkey, and it said to Bilam, 'What have I done to you that you hit me three times?' 'You've been tricking me!' said Bilam, 'If I had a sword, I'd kill you!'

"The donkey replied, 'Aren't I the donkey you've been riding for a long time? Have I ever done this before?'

"G-d then opened up Bilam's eyes, and he saw the angel.... G-d's angel said to him 'Why did you beat your donkey? ... If it hadn't stopped just now, I would have killed you and spared it.' "[40]

This story raises a number of interesting issues[41], but it certainly demonstrates an animal talking. As

---

[40] Num 22:22-33

[41] See the chapters on Rights of Magical Creatures and on Magic Wands for more on this story

we asked above, if thoughtful speech is limited to the human soul, how can this happen?

We see an answer in the Mishna[42] that teaches that "Ten things were created at twilight on the Friday of the week of creation: the mouth of the earth, the mouth of the well, the mouth of the donkey, ..." This means that when G-d had finished creating the world, in the final minutes before the first Sabbath when He rested from His creation, He created a few exceptions to the newly-created rules of nature. These are special things that G-d inserted into creation for miracles that He foresaw needing later.

The mouth of the earth refers to the ground in the Sinai desert that swallowed up the rebellious Korach and his followers[43]. According to the rules of nature ground is usually solid, and a special exception had to be built into creation for Korach's punishment to later be possible. That exception does not change the rules of nature regarding solid ground, it was a special exception. Likewise, the well that followed the Israelites in the desert to give them water was also an exception.

Thirdly, the mouth of Bilam's donkey was an exception to the general rule that donkeys – and animals in general – do not talk.

The point of this Mishna is that the general rules of nature, such as ground not opening, wells not moving, and animals not talking, remain in force, while a few exceptions are only Divinely ordained exceptions.

---

[42] Pirkei Avot 5:9
[43] Num 16:32

31

This point is made explicitly by the commentary of Rabbeinu Bechaya, who relates Bilam's donkey to the snake in the creation story, explaining that both are exceptions to the general rule of nature:

"If you look at the hidden meaning of the matter, you see that the speech of the donkey is like the speech of the snake. Neither spoke of its own accord, because neither had a speaking soul. Rather, 'and G-d opened the mouth of the donkey' is like 'and G-d opened up Bilam's eyes, and he saw the angel'[44].

Lastly, it is interesting to note that both Talmudic comments and general folklore surrounding Golems, magical people-like creatures created through Kabbalistic mystical secrets, indicates that they have fully human-like bodies but cannot speak. (Golems are discussed more in the chapter Creating Bodies.)

So on the surface it appears that Harry Potter's accounts of talking animals is inconsistent with Torah concepts. Torah tradition says that in general animals cannot speak, while the Harry Potter books describe lots of animals talking on a regular basis.

Of course, we can always imagine that House Elves are filling the role originally expected of snakes, and concoct other magical explanations for snakes, centaurs, and other talking creatures that Harry encounters. But that is a subject for a different book....

---

[44] Rabbeinu Bechaya on Numbers 22:28; see also Ibn Ezra on Gen 3:1 who also relates the snake to the donkey.

Day of Rest, Day of Magic

Bereisheet #3

At the end of the story of creation, we read about the first Sabbath (Shabbat in Hebrew, commonly "Shabbos") on the Saturday of creation:

"The sky and the earth were completed, with all they contained, and on the seventh day G-d completed all the work He had been doing. On that seventh day G-d rested from the work He had been doing. G-d blessed the seventh day and made it holy, because on that day He rested from all the work that G-d had done to create."[45]

G-d's "resting" on the Sabbath of creation, completing creation by creating the concept of resting, is the reason for the Biblical prohibition of constructive work on Shabbat:

"Remember the Sabbath day and make it holy. Work for six days, doing all your constructive work, and the seventh day is the Sabbath for G-d, do not do any constructive work, yourself, your sons and daughters, your workers and maidservants, your animals, or foreigners who have joined you, because G-d made the heavens and the earth, and the seas and everything in them, all in six days, and on the seventh day He rested."[46]

---

[45] Gen 2:1-3
[46] Ex 20:8-11

Because G-d is all-powerful, and presumably did not need to rest because of physical tiredness, Judaism understands the Sabbath not only as a day to lie around and "rest," but rather a day to stop producing and creating, to cease constructive work that adds to or changes nature, and to instead focus on spiritual and emotional pursuits. On Shabbat we stop "becoming" and focus on "being"[47]. Rather than change or build the world, we enjoy the world as it exists.[48]

Is magic considered work?

Jewish law prohibits a number of types of constructive work on the Sabbath, all of which in some way change the natural world. Because the prohibited actions are modeled after G-d's creation, the things that are prohibited are not necessarily difficult or "work-like," since nothing's hard for G-d. Rather, they are all "creative" acts, things that change or add to the natural world, as G-d did in creation. One of these prohibitions is to kindle a flame:

"You shall not kindle a flame, in any of your dwelling places, on the Sabbath day."[49]

Note that the prohibition is only kindling, and not using a flame that has already been lit. Using G-d's

---

[47] Attributed to Rabbi Matis Weinberg of Jerusalem

[48] Interestingly, the Torah says clearly in the first quote above that even though everything in the world had been created in the first six days, G-d's creation was only complete on the seventh day, because the Sabbath day is itself a necessary part of creation.

[49] Ex 35:3

creation on the Sabbath is expected; we just can't change it or add to it. Moreover, when the Torah says "flame," it is understood to include anything that produces light or heat, the word "flame" being a prototype of a broader prohibition (just as other specific actions discussed in the Torah are prototypes of general laws). Heat and light can be used on the Sabbath, but actions that produce them are forbidden. According to most authorities, this is the basis for prohibiting turning electric lights and ovens on or off on Shabbat.[50]

In the world of Harry Potter, however, wizards do not kindle flames with matches, and do not turn on lights or ovens, they get their light and heat magically, as we see clearly at the end of Sorcerer's Stone:

> ' *"Light a fire!" Harry choked.*
>
> ' *"Yes - of course - but there's no wood!" Hermione cried, wringing her hands.*
>
> ' *"HAVE YOU GONE MAD?" Ron bellowed. "ARE YOU A WITCH OR NOT?"*
>
> ' *"Oh, right!" said Hermione, and she whipped out her wand, waved it, muttered something, and sent a jet of bluebell*

---

[50] Note that the issue of electricity on Shabbat is a very complex one, and that truly understanding it requires in-depth study of both Jewish law and physics. Some Torah authorities prohibit use of electricity on the Sabbath for reasons having nothing to do with fire, such as issues in completing a circuit. The summary here is simply a bottom line according to most authorities.

flames....' (Harry Potter and the Sorcerer's Stone, chapter 16)

Interestingly, Harry's "lumos" charm seems to light up his wand even when he's not holding it, as we see in chapter one of Order of the Phoenix:

> *"... next moment, he had landed hard on the ground and his wand had flown out of his hand... Harry yelled, his eyes watering with pain as he scrambled to his hands and knees, feeling around frantically in the blackness... 'Where's - wand - come on - lumos!' He said the spell automatically, desperate for light to help him in his search - and to his disbelieving relief, light flared inches from his right hand - the wand tip had ignited."*

Which brings us to our question: Would a "lumos" spell, or Hermione's flame-producing spell, or any magical way of producing fire, light, or heat, be considered a violation of the Sabbath? Believe it or not, this question is addressed in classic Jewish Law.

The Torah's prohibition of sorcery is discussed more in the chapter on magic shows, and can be summarized as follows: The Torah prohibits Jews from doing non-Jewish sorcery, called "the ways of the Amori,"[51] but permits Jewish Kabbalistic forms of magic[52].

The Pischei Teshuva commentary[53] on the Shulchan Aruch[54] quotes an earlier book, called

---

[51] Lev 19:26,31; Deut 18:10-12; Shulchan Aruch YD 179
[52] Shulchan Aruch YD 179:15
[53] YD 179:7

Amudei Kesef, making the following amazing statement:

"People used to raise and turn a certain item in a certain way to cause a candle to ignite nicely on the Sabbath. Doing so would not violate the prohibition of kindling a fire on the Sabbath, because the person did not have contact with the candle. But it would violate the prohibition of 'following in the ways of the Amori' (i.e., sorcery), so it should not be done, even during the week."

It is not clear exactly what prohibited magical act is being described, but we can see three things from the statement of the Pischei Teshuva. First, there was some kind of technique for lighting fires that was, or was thought to be, a type of sorcery or magic. Second, the experts in Jewish law of the time decided that these actions were violations of the prohibition on non-Jewish witchcraft. Third, these magical actions were not a violation of the Sabbath, because there was no physical cause-and-effect relationship between the action and the fire (extrapolating somewhat from the phrase "did not have contact").[55]

While it is interesting to speculate on what exactly this act of magic was, we may never know.

---

[54] YD 179:15

[55] It is not clear from the Pischei Teshuva exactly why "not having contact with the candle" would make this magical fire-lighting be permitted from the perspective of Sabbath restrictions. Rabbi Yaacov Haber suggests that it is such an abnormal way to light a fire that it would not be a "melechet machshevet," a common way people think of doing things. Detailed Halachic analyses such as this require more background than this book can give, and also require more details of the action being discussed than we have.

However, the Pischei Teshuva's comment gives us an answer to our question above. Magical actions that cause light or heat might be prohibited as non-Jewish magic, but are not Sabbath violations.

The same idea[56] explains similarly how Moses was able to write thirteen Torah scrolls on the last day of his life[57] when the last day of his life is calculated to have fallen on the Sabbath.[58] Commentaries say that Moses did the writing magically, by saying a magical Name of G-d and making a quill do the writing on its own. Since this is not a natural way to write, it would not be prohibited on the Sabbath.

The same idea is also used to explain the Talmudic statement that the future Holy Temple might be built on the holiday of Passover.[59] Since the Temple will be built, or at least the final step of its building will be carried out, in a miraculous fashion, its building will not be a violation of the holiday's prohibitions.[60]

Based on all we have said, Jews are advised not to go and practice their "lumos" spells, either on the Sabbath or during the week. But we have seen that magical actions are not considered "constructive work" on the Sabbath.[61]

---

[56] Teshuvos Chasam Sofer, Likutim, chap 29

[57] Even one Torah scroll takes months to write.

[58] See Rosh commentary on Talmud Pesachim, 10:13

[59] Talmud Sukkah 41a

[60] Em HaBenim Semeicha 3:82, p444 in the English edition

[61] See Mishna Berurah 404:2 for a discussion of whether flying through the air on the Sabbath by saying a magical Name of G-d would constitute a violation of the Sabbath laws.

Rabbinic discussions of the Sabbath included things that Harry would never expect to hear outside of Hogwarts!

Noah's Care of Magical Creatures

Noach #1

When we think about Noah (Noach in Hebrew) collecting the animals to bring into the ark, most of us tend to imagine lions and tigers, cows and rams, and other "regular" animals. After all, Torah does not talk about mythical animals like those found at Hogwarts.

Or does it? Might Fawkes the Phoenix have been on Noah's ark?

The Talmud[62] tells the following Midrashic story about Noah on the ark:

"Noah found the phoenix (Hebrew: avarshina) hiding in the bottom of the Ark. He said to it, 'Don't you want food?' It replied, 'I saw you were busy, and did not want to trouble you.' He said to it, 'May it be G-d's will that you never die.' Therefore the Prophet says, 'I shall expire with my nest, and as the phoenix (Hebrew: chol), I shall increase my days.'[63]"

Rashi's commentary on the Talmud clarifies the two different Hebrew names of animals to which the Talmud refers:

---

[62] Sanhedrin 108b
[63] Job 29:18

" 'Avarshina' (is) a type of bird, called 'chol' in the terminology of the Bible, which never dies."

In modern Hebrew a phoenix is called Off Ha'chol, literally "the chol bird," and the title of The Order of the Phoenix is translated into Hebrew as Misdar Off Ha'chol.

Several commentaries[64] quote the same Midrash[65] that explains the phoenix's immortality:

"Rabbi Yannai taught: It lives for a thousand years, and at the end of this thousand years, a fire emerges from its nest and incinerates it. A volume equivalent to an egg is left, which grows limbs and lives. Rabbi Yudan taught: It lives for a thousand years, and at the end of this thousand years, its body falls apart and its wings fall off, but a volume equivalent to an egg is left, which grows limbs and lives."[66]

So we see the magical phoenix quite clearly in Torah literature! This sounds just like Dumbeldore's explanation to Harry in the middle of Chamber of Secrets (chapter 12):

> *"Fawkes is a phoenix, Harry. Phoenixes burst into flame when it is time for them to die and are reborn from the ashes."*

---

[64] Maharasha's commentary on the Talmud and Rashi's commentary on Job

[65] BR 19:5

[66] The name "chol" is the same Hebrew word as the word for "sand," which commentaries say alludes to the bird's disintegrating like sand, or that the number of years it lives are as plentiful as sand (Maharil Diskin on Gen 3:6).

Interestingly, the same Midrash gives a second, very different explanation of the phoenix's immortality:

"Eve fed the animals and birds from the Tree of Knowledge. They all listened to her, except for one bird, called the phoenix (chol), as the Bible says, 'and as the chol I will increase my days'[67]."

Since all people and animals were immortal until eating from the tree of knowledge, the phoenix's not eating from the tree of knowledge meant it would never die.

Eve's feeding all the animals from the Tree of Knowledge is alluded to by the verse "she took its fruit and ate, and she also gave some to her husband."[68] The Midrash interprets the word "also" as meaning that she had already given some to others, namely the animals.[69] The final letters of the Hebrew phrase "she took its fruit and ate," "VaTikach MiPiryo VeTochal," spell out "ch-o-l," phoenix, alluding to the phoenix's not eating from the tree's fruit.[70]

So which is the reason that the Midrashic phoenix lives forever? Is it because it did not eat from the tree of knowledge, or because of Noah's blessing?

Commentaries on the Midrash give two possibilities. One is that the Sages simply disagree, that the sage quoted in the Midrash attributes the

---

[67] Job 29:18
[68] Gen 3:6
[69] As explained by Maharil Diskin on Gen 3:6
[70] Nishmat Kol Chai, chapter on Chol, quoting Kabbalistic sources

phoenix's longevity to the Garden of Eden, and the sage quoted in the Talmud attributes it to Noah's blessing[71].

The second possibility is that the phoenix's longevity was earned in two stages. It lives a long time, and does not die a natural death like other animals, because it did not eat from the tree of knowledge. Then Noah's blessing added to its immortality, either by giving it the process of rejuvenation by burning up and being reborn, or by giving it Divine protection from hunters and accidents[72].

If all these Torah sources discuss the magical phoenix, why do we not see them nowadays? One simple possibility is that phoenixes ignite and are reborn only in remote locations, that they were spotted occasionally over the years (resulting in all the popular myths) but generally avoid being seen. Another possibility is that the phoenix's blessing for longevity ended at some point in history and they now live naturally.

Many commentaries, however, take all the Biblical and Midrashic discussions of the phoenix to be metaphorical. The Book of Job, for example, used the bird as a metaphor for long life, and did not refer to actually seeing one. Both stories from the Midrash above can be understood this way, as lessons about the importance of caring for other people's difficulties (the Midrash of Noah) and about doing the right thing in the face of a temptation (the Midrash of Eve). Each, according to the Midrash,

---

[71] Yafeh To'ar on BR 19:5
[72] Maharil Diskin on Gen 3:6

merits a lot of Divine reward, metaphorically earning long life or immortality.

Other commentaries say that the phoenix is used by our sages as a metaphor for "the soaring of the intellect, which continues even when man's body becomes weak"[73].   Others see the phoenix as a metaphor for the Jewish people throughout history, often appearing "burnt up" but always being reborn[74].

All in all, the magical phoenix has left us a lot to think about. Anyone intrigued by the existence of magical animals has no shortage of Torah sources for them.   And anyone looking for metaphors for a soaring intellect or the everlasting Jewish people need look no further.

But most importantly, we see two things that we can think about in our own lives, doing what is right when we're given a temptation not to (as in the story of Eve) and caring that others not work too hard for our own sake (the story of Noah). According to the Midrash, these are how immortality is earned, either real or metaphorical.   Even without spells or incantations, our own behavior can be as hot as a phoenix.

---

[73] Yafeh To'ar

[74] See the chapter on the Phoenix in Magical Creatures, by Rabbi Nosson Slifkin, for this and more on the magical phoenix

Owl post, Raven post, and dove post

Noach #2

Folklore about witches and wizards has always included sending mail by owls, called Owl Post in the world of Harry Potter:

> *"Just then, the mail arrived. Harry had gotten used to this by now, but it had given him a bit of a shock on the first morning, when about a hundred owls had suddenly streamed into the Great Hall during breakfast, circling the tables until they saw their owners, and dropping letters and packages onto their laps." (Sorcerers Stone, ch 8)*

And in Ron's description of the magical town of Hogsmeade:

> *"The post office, Harry! About two hundred owls, all sitting on shelves, all colour-coded depending on how fast you want your letter to get there!" (Prisoner of Azkaban, chapter 8)*

Sometimes other birds, besides owls, are used for mail:

> *"Harry had received two letters ... since he had been back at Privet Drive. Both had been delivered, not by owls (as was usual*

with wizards) but by large, brightly colored, tropical birds... they put him in mind of palm trees and white sand." (Goblet of Fire, chapter two)

Would you believe that Owl Post, or at least Bird Post, existed in the times of the Torah? Or that commentaries discuss it as a regular part of life in Biblical times?

The Torah portion of Noah, at the end of the story of the flood and Noah's ark, tells us how Noah checked whether the flood waters had receded enough to make it safe to leave the ark:

"The ark came to rest... on the mountains of Ararat.... After forty days Noah opened the window of the ark which he had made. He sent out the raven, and it kept coming and going until the waters dried from the earth. Then he sent out the dove to see if the waters had receded from the ground. But the dove couldn't find a place to rest, and it returned to the ark....

"He waited another seven days, and again sent out the dove from the ark. The dove came back in the evening with an olive branch in its beak, and Noah knew that the waters had subsided from the ground. He waited another seven days and sent the dove out, and it did not return."[75]

While we all accepted this story when we learned it as children, there are a number of details that need to be clarified:

---

[75] Gen 8:4-12

1. Why did Noah send specifically a dove and a raven, and why in that order?

2. Why would Noah risk the lives of two of the birds he had saved from the flood, which were needed to repopulate their species?

3. Why not just wait, or look out the window himself, or wait for G-d to tell them to go out of the ark?

The second question is the most significant, because risking the lives of the animals on the ark would undermine the entire project to which Noah had dedicated his life!

Rabbi Naftali Tzvi Yehuda Berlin, in his commentary Ha'amek Davar, gives a fascinating explanation. In Biblical times it was common, he says, to keep birds in the house for sending mail. As he says[76]:

"This raven and this dove weren't from the pairs that entered the ark at G-d's command to keep the species alive, rather, before the flood Noah was one of the important people whose custom it was, even then, to raise ravens and doves. The Talmud says that these animals are included in the category of 'household'[77] .... The raven in the house would be sent for not-so-long distances, and the dove was for sending letters a longer distance and bringing various objects in its mouth."

---

[76] commenting on Gen 8:7

[77] Shabbos 128a, that doves are commonly found in homes, also Baba Basra 8a that ravens are found and fed in homes

When Noah sent out the two birds, he wasn't sending out the birds that had been selected to save the species. Those he wouldn't risk, he had to save them to fulfill the Divine purpose of repopulating the world. But when Noah needed a messenger to check something and report back to him, he used his own birds, the birds that had been in his home before the flood for the purpose of sending mail and other long-distance errands.

This explains why Noah first sent the raven and then the dove. The ark had set down at the top of the hill, and he first wanted to check the short distance around the ark ("the earth"), for which the raven was the choice for the job. Second, he wanted to check a wider area ("the ground"), farther from the ark, for which the dove was better suited.

The use of birds for sending messages, particularly doves, is alluded to by other Torah sources as well. The book Nishmat Kol Chai describes doves being used for sending messages as recently as the early 20th century. Doves are attributed with both reliability and with strong powers of recognition. This is discussed by Ramban in his discussion of the power of the animal soul[78].

According to the Ha'amek Davar and these other sources, then, it appears that sending out birds was a regular part of life in Noah's time, similar to telephone calls or e-mail nowadays. In this context Noah's actions make perfect sense, and our three questions above are answered.

---

[78] Ramban commentary on Lev 17:11

We see this other places in the Bible as well. For instance, as Rashi points out[79], it was a Raven that brought food to Elijah (Eliyahu) in the desert[80].

It seems that Noah might have been very comfortable at the Hogwarts mail delivery or the Hogsmeade post office!

---

[79] on Gen 8:7
[80] Kings 1-17:6

Ghosts and curtains

Lech Lecha

At the end of Order of the Phoenix, Harry asks Nearly Headless Nick, the Griffindor house ghost, about his existence as a ghost:

> *" '...you came back, didn't you?' said Harry urgently. 'People can come back, right? As ghosts. They don't have to disappear completely. Well?' he added impatiently, when Nick continued to say nothing.*

> *" Nearly Headless Nick hesitated, then said 'Not everyone can come back as a ghost. ... Wizards can leave an imprint of themselves upon the earth, to walk palely where their living selves once trod,' said Nick miserably. 'But very few wizards chose that path.'*

> *" 'Why not?' said Harry? ... 'Listen - what happens when you die, anyway?' ....*

> *" 'I cannot answer,' said Nick. ... 'I was afraid of death, ... I chose to remain behind.... I know nothing of the secrets of death, Harry, for I chose my feeble imitation of life instead.' (Order of the Phoenix, chapter 38)*

This is an interesting notion of ghosts, that they are the souls of people who couldn't let go of this world, and choose to stay in the world even in death, as ghosts, giving up full knowledge of heavenly secrets.

Does Torah literature say anything about ghosts? Is this explanation of how people become ghosts consistent with Torah concepts?

In the Torah portion of Lech Lecha, G-d promises to Abraham (Avraham) that his descendents would receive the land of Israel (then called Canaan, or Cena'an in Hebrew). But Abraham wouldn't see this happen in his lifetime -- his grandson Jacob and his children would first go to Egypt, where they would survive slavery and only then return to the land promised to Abraham.

The Talmud, in a midrashic discussion of a dialogue years later between G-d and Moses[81], describes the following:

"G-d said to Moses, 'Go say to Abraham, Isaac, and Jacob, the oath I made to you, to give the land of Israel to your descendents, has been fulfilled for your children.'"[82]

How did G-d want Moses to give this message to Abraham, Isaac, and Jacob? Commentaries explain that he was to talk with their spirits, or souls, after his (Moses's) own death later that same day.

The Talmud records this story in the middle of a debate between the sages about whether souls of dead people are aware of what happens in the world.

---

[81] Deut 34:4
[82] Brachot 18b

51

One opinion is based on the verse[83] "His children are honored and he does not know it" which implies that the dead are disconnected from this world. The other opinion is based on the next verse[84] "his flesh pains him, and his soul will mourn for him," which implies an everlasting connection between physical events and the soul.

The story about Moses being instructed to give a message to Abraham, Isaac, and Jacob seems to indicate that the dead do not know of the events in the world, and thus the forefathers had to be told by Moses that the Jewish people had entered the land of Israel. The Talmud concludes, however, that the story is not proof one way or the other, because even if the spirits of our ancestors already knew that the Jews had entered Israel, G-d still may have wanted Moses to inform them directly that G-d's oath had been fulfilled, either out of respect for them or as a moral lesson to Moses. The Talmud therefore does not draw any conclusion from this story as to the nature of ghosts and their relationship to the physical world. Commentaries indicate in conclusion that the dead do in fact know the events of the world[85].

Until now we have been discussing souls that live on after people die, but not ghosts that exist in this world in any form. But the Talmud[86] proceeds to tell the following bizarre story, reminiscent more of a movie than of Jewish writings. Some commentaries[87] say that the story occurred in a

---

[83] Job 14:21
[84] Job 14:22
[85] Tosfos Sota 34b d.h. Avoti
[86] Brachot 18b
[87] Maharasha, Ritva

dream, but others[88] say that the Talmud is describing events that occurred in reality:

" A certain righteous man gave a dinar (a lot of money) to a poor person before Rosh HaShana (an over-generous gift) during a year of economic difficulty. His wife was frustrated and angry with him for doing it, so he went out, and found himself in a cemetery.[89]

In the cemetery he heard two spirits talking to each other. One said to the other, 'My friend, let's go wander the world, and hear from behind the curtain what bad things are going to happen.' The other replied, 'I can't, because I was buried wrapped in reeds, but you go ahead, and tell me what you hear.'

The first ghost wandered around and returned, and his friend asked 'my friend, what did you hear from behind the curtain?' He said, 'I heard that crops planted during the first rainy season will be destroyed by hail.' The man left, and planted only during the second rain, and while everyone else's crops were destroyed, his were not. "

The Talmud continues to tell that the man went back in subsequent years on Rosh HaShana night, always the night that Divine decrees for the year are decided in heaven[90]. Each year he heard what the

---

[88] Ohr Yisroel chapter 26

[89] Ohr Yisroel explains that he went to the cemetery to learn humility and anger control in the face of his wife's frustration. Some commentaries explain this as a dream because of the incongruity of a sage's going to a cemetery on Rosh HaShana night.

[90] as explained by Shita Mekubetzes

ghost said was Divinely decreed to happen, and benefited each year from the advance knowledge.

This story shows us a few interesting elements of the Talmudic perspective on ghosts. First, there are ghosts who can walk around in our world and see what people are doing, and at the same time see the mystical secrets of the world that we cannot see. This seems not to match the idea presented in Harry Potter, that people choosing to become ghosts give up their ability to see heavenly secrets. But second, there are some ghosts that somehow exist but are restricted from moving around, and cannot even leave their graves.

What is the difference between the two ghosts? Why can one roam the world and see heavenly secrets, while the other has to remain at its grave?

Most commentaries explain this in terms of a time period immediately after death, during which souls are in some way locked to their bodies and are mourning their death. The Talmud[91] says as follows:

"We see from the verse 'His flesh will be pained over itself'[92] that a person's soul mourns over his body for seven days, as we see[93] 'And he (Joseph) established mourning for his father (Jacob) seven days'[94]. Rabbi Abahu said: Everything said in the presence of a dead person is known to that person until the casket is closed (some translate 'until the headstone is placed')."

---

[91] Shabbos 152a-b
[92] Job 14:22
[93] in the Torah portion of VaYechi
[94] Gen 50:10

We see from this that there is a special connection of a soul to its body, lasting either until the casket is closed, or for seven days, or until the headstone is placed (or for other lengths of time given by other sources). During this time the soul's attention is focused on the body, and it cannot go to other places.

In the Talmud's story above, the second ghost couldn't leave the grave. The other ghost's soul had passed the various time periods, and was free both to wander the world and to Divine heavenly secrets from "behind the curtain."[95]

Note that these Talmudic quotes are the sources of many Jewish mourning customs, such as the seven-day shiva period, the unveiling, and the year-long Kaddish period.

One more point about this connection of a soul to its body's grave: Some commentaries say that this time period is difficult for people who, in their lifetime, were very focused on their bodies, but is easier for people who were more focused on intellectual or spiritual matters. This is somewhat similar to Nearly Headless Nick's theory quoted above, but in Jewish thought relates only to this short time period.[96]

---

[95] It is worth noting, as an aside, that some commentaries explain the story somewhat differently, saying that the second ghost was in fact able to leave its grave, but was embarrassed to do so, because when ghosts wander the world, other ghosts see them with the appearance of the clothes or covering in which they're buried (Shita Mekubetzes). While interesting, this is a minority opinion.

[96] See, in English, the article Immortality and the Soul, by Rabbi Aryeh Kaplan, published in the book If You Were G-d.

According to virtually all sources, after this time period, souls lose their connection to this world, and while they may know what happens in the world, they are at the same time open to heavenly secrets. Contrary to Nick's explanation to Harry, Jewish sources do not discuss a ghost's choosing to give up moving beyond this world.

In fact, the Chassidic Rebbe of the Chust dynasty teaches[97] that just the opposite is true. Being a ghost is not a matter of a wrong choice, it is a matter of Divine will. Not all souls have the option to exist in this world as a ghost, only those that G-d decides to reward or punish with the opportunity. If a soul is worthy, G-d may give it the opportunity to roam around the world and observe or help people through prayer or other means (as in the story above). The Zohar and Talmud even describe some great sages making this choice, in a desire to continue helping the world. If a soul needs atonement, G-d can force it to wander the world against its will, potentially causing damage that G-d decides is worthy of happening.

A final point concerns the Talmud's description of the ghosts as "looking behind the curtain" to see Divine secrets. This is referring to a metaphorical "curtain" that separates between this world and G-d's presence[98].

This curtain is mentioned elsewhere in the Talmud as well. For example, the Talmud[99] discusses three sins which G-d punishes "with the curtain open," i.e., with His direct unmitigated

---

[97] based on older chassidic sages
[98] Rashi on Brachot 18b
[99] Baba Metziah 59a

attention. (The primary such sin is insulting other people.) Similarly, the Talmud[100] makes the statement that when someone studies Torah despite its being difficult, G-d "keeps the curtain unlocked before him," meaning that he earns more of G-d's direct reward.

Not only ghosts can hear Divine statements from behind the curtain. The Talmud discusses a scholar turned heretic, called Acher, who had Divine visions of what the Almighty thought of his heretical actions, which he referred to as "the things that I heard from behind the curtain"[101]. Also, in the story of the Ten Martyrs, told in the Yom Kippur Mussaf prayer service[102] and summarized in the Tisha B'Av Kinot service, Rabbi Yishma'el confirms that the ten sages' martyrdom is Divinely destined, and refers to having heard this "from behind the curtain."

Even more mystically, the Talmud asks how demons can know the future, when they are presumably not privy to the Divine secrets that angels are.[103] The Talmud answers that demons, like the ghosts discussed earlier, can hear things announced from behind the curtain[104].

The Ha'amek Davar uses this idea to explain that sorcerers can sometimes explain prophetic dreams,

---

[100] Sotah 49a

[101] Chagiga 15a

[102] Page 589 in the Artscroll Yom Kippur prayerbook

[103] A full discussion of a Jewish perspective on angels and demons is beyond our scope here, but the most common approach is that G-d creates demons to carry out His negative actions in the world, and angels for the positive. The idea that demons act against G-d, against His interests and out of His control, is not a Jewish concept.

[104] Chagiga 16a

but only those dreams that reveal things that were announced behind the curtain, because they were heard by demons. But sorcerers cannot explain dreams containing secrets that G-d only revealed to a single person[105]. This is discussed more in the chapter Dreams: Divination or Digestion.

Harry Potter fans will find this concept of "curtains" familiar from the end of Order of the Phoenix when Harry and his friends are in the Department of Mysteries, in the room that Dumbeldore later calls the Death Chamber:

> *"This room was larger than the rest, dimly lit and rectangular, and the center of it was sunken, forming a great stone pit some twenty feet deep.... There was a raised stone dais in the center of the pit, on which stood a stone archway that looked so ancient, cracked and crumbling that Harry was amazed the thing was still standing. Unsupported by any surrounding wall, the archway was hung with a tattered black curtain or veil which, despite the stillness of the cold surrounding air, was fluttering slightly as though it had just been touched....*
>
> *"He had the strangest feeling that there was someone standing right behind the veil on the other side of the archway." (Order of the Phoenix, chapter 34)*

This curtain is discussed later, when Harry is back at school, talking with Luna:

---

[105] Ha'amek Davar on Gen 41:25

" 'Has anyone you known ever died?'

" 'Yes,' said Luna simply, 'my mother. She was quite an extraordinary witch, you know, but she did like to experiment and one of her spells went rather badly wrong one day. I was nine.... anyway, it's not like I'll never see Mum again, is it?'

'Er - isn't it?' asked Harry uncertainly.

She shook her head in disbelief. 'Oh, come on. You heard them, just behind the veil, didn't you? ... They were just lurking out of sight, that's all....'

Harry did not know what to say, or to think; Luna believed so many extraordinary things ... yet he had been sure he had heard voices behind the veil, too." (Order of the Phoenix, chapter 38)

Was the curtain in the Department of Mysteries an allusion to the curtain discussed in the Talmud? It seems unlikely that J.K. Rowling has heard of the Talmudic concept, but the Hebrew translation of Order of the Phoenix uses the same Hebrew word that the Talmud uses in the quotes above, "pargod," and truth has a way of spreading, so who knows...?

Whatever differences we see between the concepts of ghosts in the Talmud and in Harry Potter, or the similar descriptions of the curtain separating this world from the supernal realms, we see that these concepts aren't only the subject of stories, they are part of Jewish wisdom.

Mudbloods, Moabites & Moshiach

VaYeira #1

How important is it for a wizard (in the world of Harry Potter) to have pure wizard ancestry? This is the conflict summed up well by Harry's friend Ron in Chapter seven of Chamber of Secrets, after Hermione is called a "mudblood" by another student (in the movie this is said by Hermione herself):

> *"Mudblood's a really foul name for someone who is Muggle-born, you know, non-magic parents. There are some wizards who think they're better than everyone else because they're what people call pure-blood.... I mean, the rest of us know it doesn't make any difference at all."*

Throughout the series this debate rages on, as Dumbeldore says to the Minister of Magic at the end of Goblet of Fire (chapter thirty six) :

> *"You place too much importance, and you always have done, on the so-called purity of blood! You fail to recognize that it matters not what someone is born, but what they grow to be!"*

What do you think the Torah says about the subject?

There is a surprising attitude towards "purity of lineage" at the end of Parshas VaYeira. After G-d destroys Sodom and Gomorrah, Abraham's nephew Lot hides in a cave with his two adult-age daughters. Having seen their whole town destroyed by Divine wrath, they thought that they were the only people left alive in the whole world. The Torah describes what happened next:

"The older daughter said to the younger, 'Our father is old, and there is not any man [left alive] in the world [to marry us].... Let's give our father wine and get him drunk, ... and have children from him.'"[106]

They proceeded to carry out their plan, first the older daughter and then the younger. The Torah concludes the chapter:

"The older gave birth to a son, and called him Moav (meaning 'from the father' in Hebrew), the ancestor of the Moabites. And the younger also had a son, who she called Ben-Ami, the ancestor of the Ammonites."

This is not exactly the kind of story we expect to see in the Torah! Besides showing us Lot's family's moral depravity, why does the Torah tell us about this?

One answer lies in the role that the nations of Moav and Ammon have later in Jewish history. The book of Ruth details how Ruth, a Moabite woman, converted to Judaism and married Boaz the sage, and gave birth to the grandfather of King David. King

---

[106] Gen 19:31-33

David became the ancestor of all Jewish kings, and also of the future Messiah (Moshiach). As a Moabite, Ruth was descended from Lot's older daughter's son.

At the same time, the Book of Kings tells us that King Solomon married a woman named Naama the Ammonite, who, similar to Ruth, converted to Judaism and gave birth to King Solomon's successor. Naama, as an Ammonite, was descended from Lot's second daughter's son.

So we see an amazing thing here: Both of Lot's daughters had their descendants, from their immoral relationships with their father, included into the Jewish royal bloodline! The Moshiach will be descended on two sides from the union of Lot and his daughters! Hardly the noble bloodline that we expect!

The Midrash takes this one step further, saying that the very reason that Lot and his daughters were saved from Sodom was in order to give birth to nations that would lead to the Moshiach:

"[The angels said to Lot] 'Go, take your two daughters who are found here...'[107]. Rabbi Tuvia the son of Rabbi Isaac said, This alludes to two who were found: Ruth the Moabite and Naama the Ammonite. Rabbi Isaac said: The verse[108] says 'I found King David my servant,' where was he found? In Sodom!"[109]

---

[107] Gen 9:15
[108] Psalms 89:21
[109] Midrash BR 50:10

This Midrash is saying, in terse Talmudic style, that when the angels told Lot to take his daughters from Sodom, the reason was that Ruth and Naama had to descend from them. In other words, the immoral relationships and their consequences were actually part of G-d's Divine plan for the royal and messianic bloodline! The Midrash then identifies Sodom, the city so immoral that it had to be Divinely destroyed, as the root source of King David, the place where King David's origins can be found.

If we look more closely, we see that King David's and the Moshiach's roots in impurity go beyond Lot and his daughters. Boaz, Ruth's husband, is from the tribe of Judah. In the Torah portion of VaYeshev[110] we get a look at the early days of the tribe of Judah.

Until shortly after Talmudic times, the practice was that when a husband died without having had children, his younger brother would marry his widow (Levirite marriage) in order that the original husband's family line continue through his wife.[111] Judah, however, prevented his younger son from marrying his older son's widow, as the Torah describes:

"Judah took a wife named Tamar for his first-born son Er. But Er was evil in G-d's eyes, and he died.... And Judah told Onan [his middle son] to marry his brother's wife, to carry on his brother's family... but he did wrong in G-d's eyes, and he also died. Judah said to his daughter-in-law Tamar, 'live as a widow

---

[110] Gen Chapter 38
[111] This process was obviously only carried out with the wife's agreement, and was stopped when society changed and younger brothers stopped being able to do this with the proper motivations.

in your father's house until my [third] son Shla grows up.' He was worried that Shla would also die. Tamar went to live in her father's house, and the years went by."

The Torah continues: "After a long time, Judah's wife died, and he went to supervise the shepherds.... Tamar took off her widow's clothes, and covered herself with a veil, and sat at the entrance of the wells....

"Judah saw her and thought she was a prostitute. He turned aside to her on the road, not realizing that she was his daughter-in-law...."

The Torah continues to tell us that Tamar became pregnant from Judah, and gave birth to twins, one of whom was Peretz, the ancestor of Boaz the sage, who married Ruth and was the great-grandfather of King David.

This is amazing! Events seem to have been Divinely orchestrated so that King David's ancestry on both Ruth and Boaz's sides would come from highly ignoble circumstances. (And we haven't mentioned the questionable appearance of how Ruth and Boaz met!) This seems to hardly be fitting for a king, let alone the Moshiach!

As an aside, other sources[112] enumerate other strengths that each of the women contributed to the Messianic bloodline. Our focus on the immorality involved is not meant to degrade their other valuable characteristics. That said, we need to understand

---

[112] E.g. Megila 10b; Rabbi Yissochar Frand, quoting Rabbi Joseph Ber Soloveitchik

why events seem designed to have King David and the Messiah descend from immoral circumstances.

The Midrash[113] makes an interesting point about great people with murky ancestry:

"Who can withdraw purity from impurity? Abraham came from Terach [an idol-worshipper], Yoshiah from Ammon, Mordechai from Shimi, Israel from the nations, the messianic world from this world. Who could do this? None but G-d!"

The Midrash seems to be saying several things.

First, there is no limit to the purification that a person can achieve. No one is ever lost from morality, spirituality, or a successful and productive life. A descendent of Yehuda's relationship with his daughter-in-law can marry a descendent of Lot and his daughter, and give birth to King David and the Moshiach. G-d can always withdraw purity from impurity.

Second, G-d in fact crafts the events in the world, specifically the seemingly-improper events, to bring about His Divine purpose. Every event, every action, and every decision will be woven into G-d's plans for the world.

Third, seemingly immoral people and events may contain the building blocks for the noblest of G-d's Divine plans for the world. These building blocks are hidden in the "shells" of impurity, waiting to be released (with Divine assistance) by people who

---

[113] Bereisheet Rabba 19:1

choose to "plug in" to G-d's plan through their choices and actions.

We see these ideas in the Purim story in the book of Esther. Esther was forced to completely debase herself, going through King Achashverosh's immoral and misogynistic process of becoming queen. She had to leave her family and live in the king's brothel, and then spend her life as the wife of a non-Jewish king. And yet, when Mordechai was convincing her to plead to the king on behalf of the Jewish people, he said that "Who knows if it is just for this purpose that you became queen?"[114]. Esther proceeded to save the Jewish people, and her offspring built the second Temple (Bais HaMikdash). And, like King David and the Mashiach, it all spawned from seemingly very improper circumstances.

But why is this particularly found in the royal and messianic families? Shouldn't royal families have pure origins, and the above lessons be taught in other places? Rabbi Yehuda Leow, known as the Maharal of Prague, provides a deeper understanding of things, explaining as follows:

"The King Moshiach will be descended from other nations, as King David's line is descended from Moav and King Solomon's from Ammon. The reason is that when G-d wants to bring a new element into existence, it needs to be a new creation, different from what came before, otherwise it wouldn't be truly new. Therefore, when G-d wanted to bring the Moshiach's family into existence, He did it in a way that created a new element... specifically out of the non-Jewish nations, and the further away

---

[114] Esther 4:14

from perfection the roots were, the more the result was a new creation. That is why G-d started with Ammon and Moav, because there were no nations further from morality and perfection that Ammon and Moav.... Because of that, they are the ideal source for G-d's new creation."[115]

Other sources take this even further. The whole goal of the Moshiach is to elevate the Jewish people (and the whole world) from the immoral and violent state of the pre-Messianic world to the moral and peaceful world of the Messianic era. This will be accomplished by a person who himself came from immoral roots and achieved moral and spiritual perfection. As one commentary explains:

"Immediately before the Moshiach's arrival, the Jewish people will be in a dark and terrible state, the worst ever... and it will be the Moshiach's job to raise them to the highest levels. For him to have the power to do this, Divine providence will have it that even the Moshiach's birth will reflect transforming definitive evil to the highest spirituality. Everyone alive will know that he has the ability to similarly transform all."[116]

This is why, the Maharal says, Moses grew up in Pharoh's house, as the son of Pharoh's daughter. The redeemer of the Jews in Egypt, and the leader of the Jewish people for 40 years in the desert, had to be someone who had himself grown from an impure Egyptian environment to the highest of the Jewish prophets.

---

[115] Maharal, Netzach Yisroel Chapter 32

[116] Mi'maamakim vol 1 p. 95

Based on everything we have said, it seems that the Almighty deliberately wants some great people, with the most exalted roles, to come from less-than-noble circumstances!

Returning to our original question, we see that being a "mudblood" is not only OK, it gives someone an important ingredient for greatness that a "pure-blood" will never have: the demonstrated ability to rise from less-than-noble roots and achieve greatness. Whether this point will be shown in the Harry Potter series is up to J.K. Rowling, but we can all hope to see it soon in the real-world Moshiach, as well as in our own lives.

> *As Dumbeldore said: "It matters not what someone is born, but what they grow to be."*

Whomping Willows & Monotheistic Maples

VaYeira #2

In the beginning of Book Two, Chamber of Secrets, we're introduced to the magical Whomping Willow tree, as Harry and Ron arrive at school in Ron's father's flying car:

> *" 'Watch out for that tree!' Harry bellowed, lunging for the steering wheel, but too late -- CRUNCH.*
>
> *With an earsplitting bang of metal on wood, they hit the thick tree trunk....*
>
> *At that very moment, something hit his side of the car with the force of a charging bull.... The tree they had hit was attacking them. Its trunk was bent almost double, and its gnarled boughs were pummeling every inch of the car it could reach....*
>
> *'Can you believe our luck?' said Ron miserably... 'Of all the trees we could've hit, we had to get one that hits back!' "*
> *(Chamber of Secrets, chapter 5)*

The reason for a violent magical tree's being on the school grounds is given in Prisoner of Azkaban:

"Lupin sighed, and looked directly at Harry. 'I told you, months ago, that the Whomping Willow was planted the year I came to Hogwarts. The truth is that it was planted because I had come to Hogwarts. This house... the tunnel that leads to it... The tree was placed at the tunnel mouth to stop anyone.' " (Prisoner of Azkaban, chapter 18)

We find a Midrashic discussion of Abraham having a magical tree. When three strangers (actually angels dressed as nomads) visit Abraham's tent, the Torah describes Abraham saying to them:

"Please do not pass me by, I will bring you some water, for you to wash your feet, and you can recline under the tree."[117]

Why did Abraham go out of his way to steer the visitors to his tree? The Zohar, the classic book of mysticism written at the end of the Mishnaic era, gives the following Midrashic explanation:

"In every place Abraham lived, he planted a tree, and not a regular tree as grows everywhere, but one that would only grow in the Holy Land. This tree was able to tell who believed in G-d and who believed in idols. For someone who believed in G-d, the tree would spread its leaves over the person's head and provide pleasant shade, while for someone who believed in idols, the tree would point its leaves upwards. This served to notify Abraham, and he wouldn't stop trying to convince the person of belief in G-d.... This is why, when he invited the angels, he

---

[117] Gen 18:3-4

told them to relax under the tree, in order to check them out, as he checked everyone."[118]

In other words, while the Whomping Willow magically attacks, Abraham's tree magically gave shade to those people who were spiritually deserving because of their belief in G-d and not in idols. This was both a reward for the person sitting and an indication to Abraham of whether he should teach the person about monotheism.

The Torah alludes to this later, saying that Abraham "planted a tree in Be'er Sheva, and there he proclaimed the Name of G-d the Master of the Universe"[119]. The Talmud[120] says that the end of the verse should be understood as "there he caused others to proclaim the Name of G-d," meaning that his planting this special tree was a means of teaching others about monotheism.

How did Abraham's magical tree work? Did he put a spell on it? Was it a special magical species? The Zohar quoted above continues:

"This magic was performed for G-d's sake, and it was a manifestation of the Tree of Life.... Adam sinned through it, bringing death to the world... and Abraham elevated the world through another tree which was a manifestation of the tree of life, bringing faith in G-d to the world."

In other words, Abraham's tree wasn't an independent magical act on Abraham's part, but

---

[118] Zohar VaYeira 102b, quoted in Chok Le'Yisroel VaYeira for Sunday, and Torah Shleima on Gen 18:4

[119] Gen 21:33

[120] Sota 10a

rather, because Abraham had dedicated his life to spreading monotheism and belief in G-d, to return the world to the state of purity found in the Garden of Eden, G-d granted him a tree that had power from the tree of life from the time of creation. Even if we interpret this story metaphorically and not literally, the Zohar is teaching us that Abraham's actions earned him benefits from his property beyond the natural.

Our job in life is also to carry out G-d's plans for the world, in whatever ways fit our abilities, interests, and goals. The more we do so, the more G-d will enable the things in our life to help us. While the miracles of Abraham's days are not found nowadays, our property can still be physical manifestations of the spiritual roles in our lives.

We can see this same principle in other Mitzvot (commandments) that the Torah asks of us. For example, on the holiday of Sukkot we're commanded to "sit in Sukkot for seven days, every member of the Jewish people, in order to remember that [G-d] sat us in sukkot when He took us out of Egypt"[121].

To fulfill this mitzva, Jews build Sukka-booths every year, and spend the seven days of the holiday eating in the Sukka, and living day-to-day life as much as possible in the Sukka, to remember G-d's protection in the desert after the Exodus from Egypt.

The Chassidic Rebbe of Satmar taught[122] that just as Abraham's tree was a physical manifestation of the tree of life in the Garden of Eden, our Sukkot are

---

[121] Lev 23:42-43
[122] Divrei Yoel al haMoadim, Sukkos 7, p27

physical manifestations of the Biblical Clouds of Glory that symbolized G-d's protection of the Jewish people in the desert. If we truly internalize and believe in G-d's constant protection, and turn our sitting in a sukkah into a rededication to trust in G-d, then we'll be worthy of G-d's direct protection, analogous to the Clouds of Glory in the desert.

Of course, it is hard to relate nowadays to magical property like Whomping Willows or Abraham's tree, but the same concept applies to our property in other ways as well. We see this in a song called "HaMavdil" traditionally sung on Saturday nights after the Havdala prayer that marks the end of Shabbat:

"The One (G-d) who separates between the holy and the profane, may He forgive our sins, and increase our offspring and our money like the sand (at the beach) and the stars at night."

Why are we choosing the moments just after Shabbat to ask for more money? One explanation[123] is that by showing our willingness to stop earning money on Shabbat, and by reducing our constructive use of what we have already earned for one day and instead using it specifically for Shabbat-related activity, we show G-d that we can use the property He gives us for good things, and thereby be worthy of earning more in His eyes. Saturday night, after we end the Sabbath, is thus the perfect time to ask G-d to assist us financially, having just shown Him that we will use what He gives us properly.

---

[123] Heard from Rabbi Ahron Levitansky

If we want miraculous or magical things to happen with our property, our trees, sukkahs, or anything else, the Jewish method is not spells or enchantments. Instead, we simply need to dedicate our property to a Divine purpose. While none of us sees the kinds of magical miracles that Abraham did, we can learn the lesson of Abraham's tree, and earn Divine attention on our own property.

Everyday Magic, Everyday Miracles

Chayei Sarah #1

As all Harry Potter fans know, Harry's late arrival into the wizarding world often leaves him unaware of the every-day magic that wizarding families take for granted in their day-to-day lives. One of the particular kinds of magic that is used every day in wizard houses, but that Harry is continually amazed by, is travel:

> *"Mrs. Weasley took a flowerpot off the kitchen mantelpiece and peered inside. 'We're running low, Arthur,' she sighed... 'Ah well, guests first! After you, Harry dear!' And she offered him the flowerpot.*
>
> *Harry stared at them all watching him. 'W-what am I supposed to do?' he stammered.*
>
> *'He's never traveled by Floo powder,' said Ron suddenly.... 'He'll be alright, Mum,' said Fred. 'Harry, watch us first.' He took a pinch of glittering powder out of the flowerpot, stepped up to the fire, and threw the powder into the flames. With a roar, the fire turned emerald green and rose higher than Fred, who stepped right into it, shouted "Diagon Alley," and vanished. (Chamber of Secrets, chapter 4)*

And later, when Harry learns about two other magical forms of travel:

> " 'Where're Bill and Charlie and Per-Per-Percy?' said George, failing to stifle a huge yawn.
>
> 'Well, they're apparating, aren't they?' said Mrs. Weasley....
>
> Harry knew that apparating was very difficult. It meant disappearing from one place and reappearing almost instantly in another.
>
> '... For those who don't want to apparate, or can't, we use Portkeys. They're objects that are used to transport wizards from one spot to another at a prearranged time....'
>
> 'What sort of objects are portkeys?' said Harry curiously.
>
> 'Well, they can be anything,' said Mr. Weasley. 'Unobtrusive things, obviously, so Muggles won't go picking them up...' "(Goblet of Fire, chapter six)

Throughout the series Harry learns about various kinds of every-day magic, such as traveling, cooking, cleaning, and more. While new to Harry, these are commonplace to people growing up in the wizarding world.

The Torah describes the same casual approach to everyday magic, both for traveling and other things, in the houses of our forefathers.

In the Torah portion of Chayei Sarah we read the story of Abraham sending his servant, Eliezer, to find a suitable wife for his son, Isaac. Eliezer prays along the way for Divine assistance in his task, that a suitable wife for Isaac should do certain distinctive things so that he would be able to identify her. Indeed, he instantly sees Rebecca doing exactly the things that indicate her to be the woman he was seeking.

One strange aspect of this story is that the entire story is told twice, once when it happens and once when Eliezer recounts it to Rebecca's family:

Abraham was old, and G-d had blessed Abraham in every way.	I am Abraham's servant. G-d has blessed my master and has given him flocks and cattle, silver and gold.
Abraham said … do not take a wife for my son from the daughters of the Canaanites in the area, instead you must go to my native land.	My master made me take an oath not to find a wife for his son from the Canaanite daughters in this land, but rather to go to his father's family's house.
The servant went to Aram Naharayim … he let the camels rest on their knees outside the city beside the well.	Now today I came to the well
He prayed to the G-	I prayed to the G-d

d of Abraham … 'If I say to a girl …'	of my master … 'when a girl comes to draw water, if I say to her …'
He had not finished speaking when Rebecca appeared … [124]	I had not finished speaking to myself when Rebecca suddenly came out … [125]

Rashi explains the double telling of the story in his commentary on the phrase "I came today to the well"[126], but prefaces his explanation with a reference to a miracle that happened along the way, as follows:

"[Eliezer said] 'I came today' [meaning] today I left, and today I arrived, from here we see that the earth contracted for him (since the journey should have taken 17 days, according to other sources). Rabbi Acha said, the mundane conversation of the servants of the forefathers is more pleasing to G-d than the Torah study of the forefather's descendants, for the story of Eliezer is repeated twice in the Torah, while many essential Torah concepts are taught only through hints."

Several aspects of Rashi's commentary are puzzling and need explanation:

1. What is this magical form of travel where the earth contracts?

2. Why is Eliezer's mundane conversation more pleasing to G-d than Torah study?

---

[124] Gen 24:1-15
[125] Gen 24:34-45
[126] Gen 24:42

3. What is the connection between Eliezer's magical travel and the greatness of his mundane conversation?

4. Why does Rashi make his comment about Eliezer's mundane conversation here (24:42) instead of earlier, at the beginning of the repetition of Eliezer's story (24:34), where it would seem more appropriate?

The answer to our first question comes from the Talmud[127] that says that "There were three people for whom the earth contracted: Eliezer the servant of Abraham, Jacob our forefather, and Avishai the son of Tzeruyah..."

The Talmud's second instance of the earth's contracting is from the Torah portion of Vayetze[128], when Jacob traveled from Be'er Sheva to Charan, and then back to Mount Moriah, all before the day's sunset. The third is from the Book of Samuel[129], in which King David was saved by Avishai, who traveled from the King's palace to the land of the Philistines, also in a single day.

This magical contraction of land, called Kefitzat HaDerech in Hebrew, is prevalent in Kabbalistic and Chassidic stories. It is also mentioned as a practical occurrence in the Mishna Berurah,[130] in a discussion of traveling on the Sabbath.[131] The same concept is also implied in the Torah in other places, such as

---

[127] Sanhedrin 95a
[128] Gen 28:10-11, Rashi on Gen 28:17, Talmud Chulin 91b
[129] Samuel 2:21:16-17
[130] Mishna Berurah 404:2
[131] See the chapter titled Day of Rest, Day of Magic

when the Jewish people traveled miraculously fast while leaving Egypt.[132] In all these cases, the people undertook a long journey for Divinely ordained reasons, and G-d miraculously sped up their trip.

The book BeSimcha U'v'tov Levav[133] gives a very interesting answer to our remaining questions.

The reason that Torah study is pleasing to G-d (as Rashi said above) is that it brings us closer to Him. The more we study G-d's lessons, and the more we try to understand how He runs the world and how He wants us to live in the world, the closer we should be to Him and the more we can emulate Him in our daily lives.

So why is the mundane conversation of our forefathers' servants even more pleasing to G-d?

The households of our forefathers were pervaded by G-d's presence. We can't even imagine life in a house where G-d spoke to family members, or sent angels with messages, or performed miracles. Witnessing this kind of life, a life of complete awareness and clarity of the Almighty, would bring us closer to G-d than is even possible through Torah study nowadays.

This is why, according to BeSimcha U'v'tov Levav, Rashi says that "the mundane conversation of the servants of the forefathers is more pleasing to G-d than the Torah study of the forefather's descendants." The mundane conversation of anyone

---

[132] Rashi on Deut 1:2
[133] chapter 20

who witnessed Divinity in day-to-day life will be full of an awareness of G-d, even more than the Torah.[134]

Imagine if you were going on a trip to accomplish a task, and along the way you felt the ground contracting, and you miraculously made a seventeen day journey in a few hours. Would you mention this in an offhand allusion, like "I made the trip today?" Or would you hurry to tell everyone how amazing it was? "Check it out!" The mere fact that Eliezer took miracles like this for granted, as a natural part of day-to-day life, gives us a glimpse of a life that is full of the Divine Presence.

This is why Rashi links Eliezer's miraculous travel to the merit of his casual conversation. We do see that G-d values Eliezer's story earlier, when the Torah devotes space to the second telling of the events. But his offhand allusion to such an amazing event, and the implicit familiarity with G-d's miracles, is the true demonstration of the importance of his "mundane conversation."

There are other examples of this in the Bible as well. In the Torah portion of Lech Lecha, Hagar, Sarah's maid who became Abraham's second wife, ran away from Abraham and Sarah (then called Sarai), and was in the middle of the desert when angels appeared to her and prophesized the birth of her future son Ishmael:

"...and she fled. An angel of G-d found her by the spring of water in the desert.... He asked her 'Hagar,

---

[134] Rabbi Soloveitchik taught that we can see this also in Eliezer's prayer, which was spoken as a conversation with Someone that Eliezer knew was listening, and Who he trusted to answer.

maidservant of Sarai, from where have you come and where are you going?' And she responded, 'I am running away from Sarai my mistress.' ... And an angel of G-d said to her, 'You will conceive soon, and give birth to a son, you shall call his name Ishmael, for G-d has heard your prayer. And he will be an animal-man, his hand against everyone and everyone's hand against him, and he will oppress his brothers.' And she called the name of G-d who spoke to her 'G-d who Sees,' for she said 'Could I have seen here also, after having seen before?' "[135]

Rashi, commenting on the final sentence, explains the phrase "could I have seen here also" as follows:

"This reflects astonishment, that she hadn't understood that even in the desert she would see messengers of G-d, after having seen them before only in the house of Abraham. We know that she was used to seeing angels, because when Manoah saw an angel one time he expected to die, but Hagar saw four angels and did not tremble."

Rashi's reference to Manoah is from the beginning of the story of Samson[136]. An angel appeared to prophesize Samson's birth, very analogously to the story of Hagar above. But Manoah wasn't used to seeing angels, and thought he would die as a result until his wife explained otherwise.

The stories of Eliezer and Hagar show us that in Abraham's house mystical events were commonplace, and members of his household got used to these events and took them as a matter of

[135] Gen 16:6-13

[136] Judges 13:20-25, read in the Haftara of the Torah portion of Naso

course. Others, however, were shocked or scared of these things.

We all live nowadays in a world with few overt miracles. We can see G-d's hand in nature, but do not see direct evidence of His activity in the world, like angels or supernatural travel. But if we really work on improving our belief in G-d and His control over the universe, and learn from the lessons of Eliezer and Hagar, we can know that anything we see, natural or supernatural, likely or unbelievable, is G-d's hand in the world.

We may never get as used to magic as Harry does, since we do not see it, but can our faith come close? We can only try.

Nicolas Flamel and the Children of Ketura

Chayei Sarah #2

The first Harry Potter book introduces the Philosopher's Stone, renamed The Sorcerer's Stone in the U.S. editions of the book and movie. The stone itself is described in chapter 13:

> *"The ancient study of alchemy is concerned with making the Sorcerer's Stone, a legendary substance with astonishing powers. The stone will transform any metal into pure gold. It also produces the Elixir of Life, which will make the drinker immortal.*
>
> *"There have been many reports of the Sorcerer's Stone over the centuries, but the only Stone currently in existence belongs to Mr. Nicolas Flamel, the noted alchemist and opera lover. Mr. Flamel, who celebrated his six hundred and sixty-fifth birthday last year, enjoys a quiet life in Devon with his wife, Pernelle (six hundred and fifty eight)."*

Note that Harry Potter and the Sorcerer's Stone was published in 1997, putting Flamel's birth at around the year 1332.

The folklore of Nicolas Flamel and the Philosopher's Stone wasn't invented for the Harry

Potter stories, it has been part of the legends of Alchemy for hundreds of years. Alchemy fans say that Nicolas Flamel actually existed, and lived from 1330 to 1418.

The legend of Nicolas Flamel as alchemist has also appeared in other modern novels, such as The DaVinci Code, which lists Flamel as a leader, from 1398 to 1418 (chap 79), of a secret society that possessed, among other things, "the alchemic power to turn lead into gold, and even cheat G-d by creating an elixir to postpone death" (chap 8). Sound familiar? (The DaVinci code also includes a playful jibe at Harry Potter in chapter 38.)

Interestingly, books of Alchemy legends quote "The Testament of Nicolas Flamel," reportedly published in London in 1806, saying that Nicolas Flamel learned how to make the philosopher's stone from a book of Kabbala that revealed secrets of "Abraham the Jew." Fans of the Alchemy legends have tried unsuccessfully to identify Jewish mystics named Abraham from the 1300's that fit the legend's description.

From the Torah's perspective, there is no reason to believe that any of the Alchemy legends are true. At the same time, we can speculate about Jewish mystical books that can be attributed to "Abraham the Jew," that could have inspired the Philosopher's stone legend.

In the Parsha of Chayei Sarah we see Abraham setting his affairs in order as he approaches his own death, arranging for his son Isaac's future and for the children he had with Ketura, the wife he married after Sarah's death. The Torah tells us as follows:

"Abraham gave all that he had to Isaac. To the children of his other wife he gave gifts, and then he sent them away from Isaac, to the east, to the land in the east"[137].

If Isaac was given "everything," what were the "gifts" given to the children of Ketura? Rashi explains as follows:

"Our Rabbis explained, he gave them a name of G-d (meaning a Divine incantation) for impure uses"[138].

Commentaries on the Talmud explain this "name of G-d for impure uses" as "secrets of magic and powers of demons"[139]. The Daas Zekeinim[140] explains this as "names of demons that are enlisted to do whatever their masters say." The Daas Zekeinim also points out that the Hebrew word that the Torah uses for "gifts" is spelled unusually, and has the numeric "gematria" value equal to the phrase "taught them to enlist demons" (in Hebrew "limdam le'hashbia shedim," with gematria value 890).

The Maharasha's commentary on the Talmud says that Abraham learned black magic only to be able to defend against it, not to use it. Similarly, the Maharal[141] says that Abraham taught these secrets to the children of Ketura only for defense (making Abraham perhaps the first teacher of defense against the dark arts).

---

137 Gen 25:5-6
138 Rashi on Gen 25:6, based on Talmud Sanhedrin 91a
139 Rashi on Sanhedrin 91a
140 on Gen 25:6
141 Gur Aryeh on Gen 25:6

Other sources, however, discuss Abraham's knowing and using Jewish mystical secrets. Abraham is credited as the source of the mystical secrets of the Sefer Yetzira, the Book of Creation. Sefer Yetzira gives meditative techniques for mystical healing, creating new bodies, teleportation, and more.[142] Sa'adia Gaon writes that our text of Sefer Yetzira was written in Talmudic times, but the methods taught in the book date to Abraham. The last section of Sefer Yetzira itself describes "Abraham our father" making use of these meditative secrets to bring new creatures to life:

"And when our father Abraham looked, saw, understood, probed, engraved, and carved, he was successful in creation, as the Torah writes, 'and the souls that they made in Haran'[143]."[144]

The usual explanation of Genesis 12:5 is that Abraham and Sarah had spread the knowledge of monotheism, bringing people's souls closer to G-d, not that they had actually created new people. But the Sefer Yetzira's interpretation is, if anything, even more consistent with the words of the Torah, and identifies Abraham among the early practicing mystics.

Rabbi Aryeh Kaplan's extensive English commentary on Sefer Yetzira notes that Abraham lived in the 18th century BCE, the same time period in which mystical books, such as the Vedic

---

[142] The meditative techniques listed are discussed in the chapter on Creating Bodies.

[143] Gen 12:5

[144] Sefer Yetzira, 6:7 in Vilna Gaon edition, 8:5 in Saadia Gaon Edition

Scriptures, were written in the Far East, making it logical that Jewish mystical texts would also have been written or conceived at that time.

While some commentaries indicate that "The land to the east" might be Arab areas just to the East of the Land of Israel[145], most understand this to be referring to the Far East.

Jewish tradition is not clear on whether Abraham taught the Children of Ketura the secrets of Sefer Yetzira or other mystical secrets. But the Zohar tells the following revealing story:

"Rabbi Abba said: I once was in a town where the children of the east live, and they taught me some of their ancient wisdom and showed me their books of wisdom.... I said to them, my children, all of this is similar to what we have in our Torah, but you should avoid these books, to avoid idolatry.... The ancient children of the east possessed a wisdom which they had inherited from Abraham, who had imparted it to the children of his other wife... in time they followed that wisdom to many false roads."[146]

Whatever books the Zohar is referring to, we see the Talmud and Zohar presenting a consistent connection between Jewish teachings and Eastern mysticism, brought east by the children of Ketura.

Interestingly, modern research is uncovering connections between far-East schools of thought and

---

[145] Daas Zekeinim on Gen 25:6

[146] Zohar VaYeira paragraphs 80-89 (in other editions, pages 99a-100a), Torah Shleima English Edition on Gen 25:6; see also Torah Shleima's extensive note in Hebrew Edition on Gen 25:6

Torah. One example is an article in the Journal of Chinese Medicine, issue 70, in October 2002, titled "Tefillin: An Ancient Acupuncture Point Prescription for Mental Clarity." In this article, Dr Steven Schram finds a connection between the placement of Tefillin (Phylacteries), which Jewish men wear every day during morning prayer, and the exact points on the head, arm and hand used by Chinese acupuncture to "elevate the spirit and clear the mind." According to acupuncturists, the point on the head where Tefillin is placed apparently corresponds to "Tianting (Courtyard of Heaven)," a point whose stimulation is said to calm the mind and balance the spirit, and the point on the arm in which Tefillin is placed apparently corresponds to "Tianfu LU-3 (Heavenly Residence)," one of a group of points called "Window of Heaven" said to have spiritual benefits.

Not only does Chinese acupuncture promote pressure or needles on the exact points on which Tefillin are wrapped, but some practitioners promote treatment of the arm and head before the hand, consistent with the Jewish process of putting tefillin first on the arm, then on the head, and only then on the hand. These practitioners see the points on the hand as "multipliers" that increase the effectiveness of the points on the arm and head.

The author of the article concludes "If someone handed an acupuncturist the above point formula (the places where Tefillin are placed) and asked what is being treated, there is little doubt that mental and 'shen' (spiritual) issues would be a strong part of the pattern. What is surprising is that such a point formula would be found in a non-Chinese procedure that has been continuously practiced for many thousands of years.... It seems clear that putting on Tefillin is a unique way of stimulating a very precise set of acupuncture points that appears designed to clear the mind and harmonize the spirit."

Rephrasing this from a Jewish perspective, it seems clear that Chinese schools of thought have built their acupuncture techniques on knowledge that overlaps with the Torah.

Whatever we may think of acupuncture or far-Eastern medicine or science (and this book is not meaning to promote it), it is interesting to see an overlap between Torah and Eastern schools of thought that modern scholars are unable to explain. It would be pure speculation to suggest that that this knowledge may have been brought East by the Children of Ketura, but overlap between far-Eastern thought and Torah is certainly consistent with the Torah's and Zohar's accounts.

Returning to our discussion of the legends of Nicolas Flamel, we obviously have no way of knowing whether the legends are rooted in a book of mysticism that Abraham taught the children of Ketura. There are, however, similarities between diagrams attributed to Nicolas Flamel and diagrams found in many editions of Sefer Yetzira.

Regardless of whether the legends of the Philosopher's stone are based on mystical knowledge from the children of Ketura, we see clear connections between Jewish kabbalah and far-eastern knowledge. If we're impressed or intrigued by far-east mysticism, we should stop and think: Eastern teachings may have derived from Abraham's wisdom!

When One Rises, the Other Will Fall

Toldot

The end of The Order of the Phoenix presents us with a fateful prophecy:

> *"The one with the power to vanquish the dark lord approaches... born to those who have thrice defied him, born as the seventh month dies... and the dark lord will mark him as his equal, but he will have power the dark lord knows not... and either must die at the hand of the other for neither can live while the other survives...."* *(Order of the Phoenix, chapter 37)*

This prophecy says that Harry and Voldemort are destined to battle each other until one of them kills the other. Harry represents good, Voldemort represents evil, and the eternal fight between good and evil will carry on in them until one is victorious.

Harry is understandably shocked, but not at the fact that he is somehow the embodiment of good in its battle against evil. Rather, Harry is bothered that his life must end with his killing, or being killed by, the evil Voldemort:[147]

---

[147] This is similar to Rashi's explanation of Jacob's fear in Gen 32:8: "Frightened that he would be killed, and distressed that he would kill others."

"Perhaps the reason he wanted to be alone was because he had felt isolated from everybody since his talk with Dumbeldore.... he could not muster any great sense of fear.... it was still very hard to believe as he sat here that his life must include, or end in, murder...." (Order of the Phoenix, chapter 38).

Parshas Toldos paints a similar, yet also different, picture of the role of the Jewish people in history. In the Torah, the eternal struggle is embodied in Jacob and Esav (Esau), Jacob's twin brother. Even in the womb they were in conflict:

"Rebecca conceived. The children struggled within her ... and she went to seek out [an explanation from] G-d. G-d said to her 'Two nations are in your womb, two kingdoms will separate from you. Dominance will pass from one to the other, and the elder (Esav) will serve the younger (Jacob).' "[148]

Rashi explains the phrase "dominance will pass from one to the other" in a way that sounds strikingly familiar:

"They will never be equal in greatness, when one rises, the other falls."[149]

Sound familiar?

In a sense, the eternal struggle between Jacob and Esav is a lot like the (fictional) prophesized battle between Harry and Voldemort. One of them will

---

[148] Gen 19:21-23
[149] Rashi on Gen 19:23

always dominate the other. Esav will do well precisely when Jacob does not. And ultimately one will defeat the other.

Unfortunately this destined conflict can be seen throughout history. The Jewish people, descendants of Jacob, are always either dominating, with contributions to society that far outpace our numbers, or dominated, victims of pogroms or other discrimination. The Western world, descendants of Esav, either oppresses the Jews or benefits from the Jewish contributions to society. There is rarely a middle ground.

There is, however, an important difference between the eternal struggles between Jacob & Esav and Harry & Voldemort.

At the end of the Parsha we see Isaac their father giving them the blessings that will define their lives in the same fashion. Isaac's blessing to Jacob says as follows:

"May the L-rd give you the dew of the heavens and the fat of the land, and abundant grain and wine"[150]

Rashi comments on this as follows:

"Why did he say 'the L-rd' [which is the name of G-d representing judgment, not mercy] ? It was to say, according to strict judgment: if you deserve it, He will give it to you, but if not, He will not give it to you. But to Esav he said 'the fat of the land will

---

[150] Gen 27:28

be your dwelling"[151] regardless of whether he will be righteous or wicked."

Esav's complete blessing, a few verses later, is as follows:

"The fat of the land will be your dwelling, and the dew of the heavens above. You will live by your sword, and work for your brother, but when you are pained, you may remove his yoke from your neck."[152]

Rashi explains this consistent with his previous explanations:

"When Jacob's descendants will transgress the will of G-d, and you will have a valid claim to be pained over his blessing (since Jacob's blessing above was made conditional on being righteous), you may remove his yoke."

While Jewish history has its share of military conflicts, the Torah describes the essence of the conflict between Jacob and Esav, Jew and Gentile, as spiritual rather than military. While we fight when we need to, our mission is to be a 'light unto the nations,' to influence the world through morality, ethics, and spirituality. When Jews act morally, we will succeed in influencing the world and having control, but when we do not we end up being dominated and weak.

This idea fits Rashi's commentary (quoted above) explaining the two fetuses struggling in Rebecca's womb: "They were fighting over the rights to the

---

[151] Gen 27:39
[152] Gen 27:39-40

two worlds (the physical world and the spiritual world)"[153]. The eternal struggle between Jacob and Esav is not to kill or enslave each other, it is over the relationship between the physical and the spiritual. And as Rashi also said, the condition of success is not military, but rather whether the Jews do the will of G-d.

So would-be Jewish Harry Potters can take consolation. We may be destined to represent forces of good struggling with evil in the world, but the battle will not necessarily force us to murder. Moral, ethical, and spiritual behavior will lead us to our prophesized victory.

---

[153] Rashi on Gen 19:22

Destiny and Decisions

Vayetze #1

The Hogwart's sorting hat exists for a once-a-year purpose: to read students' potentials from their heads and sort them into school houses. Gryffindor House is for the brave, Ravenclaw for the smart, Hufflepuff for the reliable, and Slytherin for the ambitious.

Some students may be hard to categorize, such as Harry, who had elements of Slytherin, or Hermione, who had elements of Ravenclaw, but both of whom were best in Gryffindor. Some students may not have their potential expressed until later, like Neville, whose Gryffindor-worthy bravery is not seen until the end of Order of the Phoenix. But the sorting hat is still trusted to see the students' destined potential.

Dumbledore, however, has a different perspective on measuring someone's potential, as he says at the end of Chamber of Secrets:

> ' "I should be in Slytherin," Harry said....
> "The sorting hat could see Slytherin's power in me, and it...."
>
> "...put you in Gryffindor," said Dumbeldore quietly.... "You know why that was. Think."

"It only put me in Gryffindor," said Harry in a defeated voice, "because I asked not to go in Slytherin...."

"Exactly," said Dumbeldore, beaming once more. "... It is our choices, Harry, that show who we truly are, far more than our abilities." '

Many people tend to think of belief in pre-destiny as the "religious" belief, and belief in self-determination as the "secular" belief. Indeed, the Talmud makes some strong statements about destiny, such as:

"Everything is predestined except a person's fear of heaven"[154]

This is derived from a verse in the Torah portion of Ekev:

"And now, Israel, what does G-d demand of you, only to fear G-d, to go in His ways, to love Him, and to serve G-d with all of your heart and soul."[155]

But the Torah portion of Vayetze presents us with a striking counterpoint. Jacob (Yaakov) is running away from his home, to avoid being killed by his brother Esav (Esau), and travels to the house of his uncle Lavan, where he meets Lavan's daughters Rachel and Leah. He falls in love with Rachel, but Lavan tricks him into marrying both of them.[156]

---

[154] Brachot 33b, Megila 25a
[155] Deut 10:12
[156] Gen 29:16-30

In describing Rachel and Leah, the Torah says that Leah was "weak-eyed." Rashi gives a Midrashic explanation of this:[157] Rachel and Leah originally looked completely alike. It had been Divinely pre-destined that Rachel would marry Jacob (the younger siblings) and Leah would marry Esav (the older siblings). Leah knew this, and was so distraught by the idea of marrying the evil Esav that she cried so hard that her eyes were permanently weak-looking. G-d heard her crying and changed her destiny to instead marry Jacob. The Midrash concludes by saying that "Prayer is so strong that it can cancel a Divine decree."

This Midrash is hard to understand. How did Leah's crying change her destiny? If that marriage had been destined, how did crying change it? More to the point, what is Divine destiny if it can be changed?

Rabbinic commentaries[158] suggest that Leah's tears reflected not only her feelings of sadness, but her determination to change herself to be worthy of a changed fate. Leah's crying wasn't only "Why me?" but "What can I do, I'll do anything!" G-d saw this and decided that she was indeed worthy of a new destiny. The original Leah was fated to marry Esav, but the changed Leah had a new destiny.

This gives all new meaning to calling someone "a changed person." The decisions we make to change our character, to make ourselves better people, and obviously the changes in our behavior and actions

---

[157] Rashi on Gen 29:17; Talmud Baba Basra 123a; Midrash Bereisheet Raba 70:16

[158] Heard from Rabbi Ahron Levitansky

that grow from these decisions, do in fact make us new people, worthy of new fate and new destiny.

The Talmudic statement quoted earlier, that everything is in the hands of heaven except the fear of heaven, now fits perfectly with the Midrash about Leah's fate. Leah's fate was always in the hands of heaven, subject to Divine destiny. But when Leah changed herself, improving her fear of heaven through her prayer and cries to G-d, the "hands of heaven" changed her fate as a result.

The idea that repentance and self-improvement make us "new people" is found explicitly in the Midrash[159] discussing the sacrifices brought on Rosh HaShana. The Torah says that on Rosh HaShana "you shall make a holy day, and do no work, and have a day of shofar-blowing. You should make the sacrifice...."[160]. The Midrash notes that the description of every other holiday says that the sacrifices should be "brought," and only for Rosh HaShana the Torah says that the sacrifice should be "made"[161]. The Midrash notes that the word "made" is used in the story of creation[162], and interprets this homiletically as saying that our Rosh HaShana observance can "make" us into new people. In the words of one midrash, G-d is saying to us "If you repent during the days between Rosh HaShana and Yom Kippur, I will credit you on Yom Kippur as a brand new creation."

---

[159] Talmud Yerushalmi Rosh HaShana 4:8, Pesichta Rabati ch 40, Pesichta D'Rav Kahana ch 23; see Torah Shleima on Num 29:2; see also Baal HaTurim on Num 29:2.

[160] Num 29:1-2

[161] The usual Hebrew word is "hikravtem," and for Rosh HaShana the Hebrew word is "asitem."

[162] Gen 1:7

The idea that repentance can change our destinies is also found in our prayers on Yom Kippur: "Repentance (decisions to change our incorrect behavior), prayer (wishing for change), and charity (deeds that actualize our self-improvement) change the evil decree." Even things that are decreed in heaven can be changed through the choices we make.

This notion of changing destinies even has practical ramifications. Rabbi Moshe Shternbuch was asked about the propriety of Jews having their palms read, based on Jewish mystical teachings that a person's destiny can be seen in his palms. He wrote in his answer[163] that on a practical level he did not believe that modern day palm readers use true Kabbalistic secrets, and thus they should not be believed. More than that, however, he said that even if Jews could find out the true destinies written on their palms, this should only be used as advice for self-improvement, because every Jew can always rise above his or her destinies and accomplish greatness beyond what is destined.

As Dumbledore said:

> *"It is our choices that show who we truly are, far more than our abilities."*

---

[163] Teshuvos ve'Hanhagos vol 1 chapter 454

Magic Wands

Vayetze #2

In the world of Harry Potter, magic requires a wand. We do see a few examples of magic without a wand, such as Harry's accidental magic in the Dursleys' house, but even the most accomplished wizards cannot do serious magic without a wand. The powerful but evil Voldemort says this explicitly:

> *"Voldemort laughed softly... 'I was as powerful as the weakest creature alive... and every spell which might have helped me required the use of a wand...' "* (Goblet of Fire)

Also, people thrown out of wizard school, who are not fully trained wizards, similarly are not allowed wands, as we see in a conversation between Hagrid and the wandmaker:

> *" 'Good wand, that one. But I suppose they snapped it in half when you got expelled?' ... 'Er, yes, they did, yes... I've still got the pieces, though....' 'But you don't use them?' ... 'Oh no, sir....' Harry noticed he gripped his pink umbrella very tightly as he spoke."* (Sorcerer's Stone)

Many people would say that wands do not play a role in the Torah or in Jewish stories of kabbalah and

101

mysticism. We'll see, however, that wands indeed play a behind-the-scenes role in miraculous events (analogous to magic) throughout the Torah, and are discussed by Chassidic masters and other kabbalists.

The Torah portion of Vayetze[164] has a story about Jacob (Yaacov) using wands ("sticks") for magic, in his business dealings with Laban, who had been trying to avoid paying him for his work:

"He (Laban) said 'What shall I give you?' And Jacob said ... 'I will resume caring for and guarding your flocks, and let me pass through all your cattle and remove any speckled or spotted lamb, and they will be my wages.'

"And Laban agreed.

"... Jacob then took soft white rods of poplar and hazel and chestnut. He peeled white stripes in them, laying bare the white of the rods. He then set the rods he had peeled in the areas where the flocks came to drink, facing the flocks, that the cattle would see them when they drank, and would give birth to speckled and spotted offspring.

"... He became exceedingly prosperous...."

What is going on here? How is Jacob magically changing the natural process of genetics? What are the rods (wands) accomplishing?

To make the question even stronger, it appears that wands were not only used in Jacob's magical activities, but that virtually any time the Torah

---

[164] Gen 30:31-43

describes a person doing magical acts, somehow bringing about a miraculous change in nature through his own actions, the person has a wand, a staff, or a stick, somehow involved in the magical act:

1. Jacob's use of wands with Laban's sheep

2. When Moses did magic in front of Pharaoh, turning his staff into a snake, to convince him of G-d's power and bring about the exodus from Egypt, and when Pharaoh's sorcerers did the same thing in response[165].

3. When Aaron started the first, second, and third of the ten plagues, and when Moses started the seventh and eighth[166], each by raising his staff in the air. Note that in several cases G-d's command was to raise their hands, but Moses and Aaron understood implicitly that they had to raise their staffs[167].

4. When Moses brought about the splitting of the sea[168], again by raising his staff in the air.

5. Twice when Moses brought water from a rock in the desert[169]. The first time G-d told Moses to bring his staff and hit the rock with it. The second time is even more notable, because G-d told Moses to bring his staff, yet did not want him to use it (and actually punished him for hitting the rock with it), making it clear that the mere presence of his staff was significant.

---

[165] Ex 4:2-5, Ex 7:9-13
[166] Ex 7:17-20, Ex 8:1, Ex 8:12-13, Ex 9:23, Ex 10:13
[167] Ibn Ezra on Ex 9:22, Ha'amek Davar on Ex 9:23
[168] Ex 14:16
[169] Ex 17:5, Num 20:11

6. When the Jews fought with Amalek in the desert, and miraculously won the battles whenever Moses's hands were raised towards heaven, and lost whenever his hands were not raised, where Moses made a point of deliberately holding his staff in his hand at the time[170].

7. After Korach's rebellion, when G-d caused Aaron's staff to blossom and grow almonds, to indicate that he was G-d's selected leader[171].

8. When Pinchas grabbed a spear to kill the rebels Zimri and Kozbi[172], about which the Baal Shem Tov[173] says the spear itself gave Pinchas prophecy to know that he was doing the right thing and that his thinking was clear-headed[174].

9. In Joshua's conquest of the land of Israel, when G-d told him that the Jews would be victorious in war when he raised his spear[175].

10. When G-d made Bilam's donkey speak to him[176] only after Bilam hit it with a stick, not after he hit it with his hands. (This story is presented in more detail in the chapters Snakes, Speech, and Souls and Rights of Magical Creatures.)[177]

---

[170] Ex 17:9-12

[171] Num 17:20-24

[172] Num 25:7

[173] in his commentary on the end of Parshas Balak

[174] based on a Kabbalistic analysis of the letters of the Hebrew word for spear

[175] Joshua 8:18, 8:26

[176] Num 22:27-28

[177] The author has not yet found a commentary that connects the speaking to the stick, but Kabbalists report ancient sources

11. When the prophet Elisha is asked to bring a dead boy back to life, and suggests that his assistant accomplish the feat himself by placing Elisha's staff next to the boy[178].

12. In Parshas VaYishlach, when Jacob refers to having left the Land of Israel (running away from Esav) as "crossing the Jordan river with only my staff"[179]. Rashi explains this by quoting a Midrash that Jacob had used the staff to magically split the Jordan river to cross, similar to Moses and Joshua.[180]

We see, then, a dozen examples of wands, staffs, sticks, or rods being used in the Torah to accomplish magical miracles!

Many commentaries give explanations of how some of these miracles worked. For example, in the story of Jacob and Laban's sheep, many commentaries have gone into depth explaining the genetic processes by which Jacob's sheep became spotted, as a highly unlikely but natural process. As another example, in the war against Amalek (number 6 above), the Mishna[181] says that "Did Moses's hands win the war? Rather, the Jews would look at Moses's hands (and see the sky), and their thoughts would turn to their Father in heaven." In other words, the battle was won by G-d's Divine

---

saying that Bilam's stick contained a parchment with G-d's name on it.

[178] Kings 2:4:29-31, in the Haftara for Parshas VaYeira; see also Talmud Pesachim 68a and Maharasha's commentary

[179] Gen 32:11

[180] Rashi on Gen 32:11 "Ki BeMakli", see also Yalkut Shimoni, and Torah Shleima on Gen 32:11

[181] Rosh HaShana 29a Mishna 3:8

assistance, which He gave whenever the Jewish soldiers thought about Him as the source of their strength. But explanations such as these leave open the question of why in all these cases there had to be sticks or staffs present at the time.

There are also several sources that link the wands, staffs, or rods mentioned above with miracles in general. Some commentaries draw analogies between some of our examples above and Moses's staff in particular. [182] The Passover Haggada specifically links the "signs" of G-d's power that were shown in Egypt to Moses's staff[183]. Similarly, Onkolus's interpretive translation to Aramaic translates "the staff of G-d"[184] as "the staff by which G-d worked miracles," similar to the phrasing found in the Passover Haggadah.

The Ha'amek Davar[185] strengthens the connection between Moses's staff and miraculous events in general. During and shortly after the Exodous from Egypt, he writes, Moses kept his staff with him at all times, because G-d was making miracles occur all the time. But towards the end of the Jews' forty

---

[182] The Vilna Gaon, in his analogy between Jacob's experiences in Lavan's house and the Jewish slavery in Egypt, relates Jacob's wands to Moses's staff (commentary on Tikkunei HaZohar chapter 3, discussedand quoted in MiMa'amakim vol 1 chapter 28). The Chassidic master Rav Nachman of Breslov (Likutei Moharan Tinyana 8:3) relates Pinchas's spear to Moses's staff, based on the verse "And Pinchas arose and executed judgment" (Psalms 106:30), observing that the word "executed judgment" is an acronym for the phrase "and (Aaron) threw (Moses's staff) before Pharaoh and it became a serpent" (Ex 7:10).

[183] in the section elaborating on Torah verses just before the listing of the plagues

[184] Ex 7:9

[185] on Num 20:8

years in the desert, as the Jews were preparing for a more natural lifestyle in the Land of Israel, and miracles were less frequent, Moses stopped carrying his staff with him. This is why G-d specifically had to tell Moses to take his staff with him when a miracle was going to occur. This underscores the general connection between wands (or staffs, or rods) and miracles.

What are all these wands accomplishing?

The book HaKsav Ve'ha'kabalah presents the first two parts of our answer.[186] First, the story of Jacob and the sheep took place after Jacob's prophecy in which G-d says that He will watch over Jacob and "be with him."[187] So it had already been decreed that Jacob would have Divine assistance while at Laban's house. In all of our other examples as well, the outcomes of the wand use had also been previously decreed by G-d.

Second, Divine decrees can sometimes be nullified by subsequent Divine decrees. Locking in a decree, so that it won't be reversed, requires a physical action. [188] This is what Jacob accomplished using the wands. The "magic" came from G-d, but Jacob initiated it and locked it in through the physical actions of the wands.[189]

But why wands?

---

[186] Commenting on Gen 30:37

[187] Gen 28:15

[188] This same concept is discussed by Ramban, commenting on Gen 12:6

[189] Em HaBanim Semeicha (chapters 2 and 3) uses this concept to explain why the miraculous launch of the Messianic era has to be preceded by natural settling of the land of Israel.

The Ba'al Shem Tov, the founder of the Chassidic movement in the 1700's, gives a mystical (and somewhat mathematical) answer. Like many of the Baal Shem Tov's teachings, fully understanding this answer requires extensive background in Kabbala (Jewish mysticism). The Baal Shem Tov, however, taught certain kabbalistic concepts in a way that a broad audience could understand and enjoy.

The Baal Shem Tov relates Jacob's wands to the starting point of G-d's creation of the universe. Before creation, there was no such thing as the 3-dimensional world as we know it. There was no up and down, north and south, right and left. There was only G-d, and G-d is not three dimensional, G-d has no physical dimensions (others say G-d is infinitely dimensional). As Rambam (Maimonides) writes:

"Since G-d has no body, he also has none of the physical attributes associated with a body: no nearness or farness, no location or size, no up or down, no right or left...."[190]

When G-d created the universe, He first had to create the 3-dimensional universe itself, even before creating the planets and other "stuff" that would be in the universe. This creation was the only example in history of creation of something from nothing, called Ex Nihilo in Latin. In Hebrew this Ex Nihilo creation is referred to as "Yesh Mi'Ayin," something (yesh) from (mi) nothing (ayin). The Baal Shem Tov says that the first step of Ex Nihilo creation is creating the concept of three dimensions.

---

[190] Rambam Yisodei HaTorah 1:11

According to the Baal Shem Tov, G-d first, in Kabalistic terms, constricted Himself to create an area in which to build a three-dimensional universe. This is referred to in kabalistic texts as "the constriction," in Hebrew as "Tzimtzum." Inside this area He then created the three-dimensional universe. G-d first created the first dimension, width, which mathematicians now call the X axis, going from right to left. He then created the other dimensions, height and depth, the Y and Z axes. The most significant of these creative steps was creating the first of the dimensions, because it established the concept of a physical universe, of dimensions. After G-d had created only this first dimension, the entire universe was in the form of a single line, with width (from right to left), but no height or depth (since height and depth hadn't been created yet).[191]

A straight line, the Baal Shem Tov continues, always symbolizes this first dimension created by G-d, the first step in creating the physical universe. The symbolism of straight lines taps into the Divine power of G-d's creation of something from nothing. This is the symbolism of Jacob's sticks/wands, which tapped into the power of G-d's original creation of our 3-dimenional universe, and channeled some of that power of creation to magically "create" a change in nature, as promised by G-d.[192] This also appears to be the symbolism of all of our other examples of

---

[191] Note that the Baal Shem Tov does not say that the universe ever existed with only one dimension, or that G-d actually created the dimensions in stages, but that conceptually the most significant step in the creation of three-dimensional space is creating the first dimension, which theoretically results in a universe in the form of a line.

[192] Kabbalists also report ancient sources ascribing similar symbolism to the beams used to build the Tabernacle, but the author has not found sources to support this.

wands, rods, staffs, or sticks being used to bring about miracles, not doing magic themselves but rather channeling the power of G-d's creation.[193]

Many of the examples we listed above have other connections to G-d's creation of the universe.

In our first example, the Baal Shem Tov notes that Jacob stripped the bark from his wands to expose the white wood underneath, which represented the light of creation. This light is the special light created on the first day of creation, even before the creation of the sun on the fourth day of creation, that the Talmud says was kept aside by G-d for Divine use[194]. Just like the shape of a wand symbolizing the first step of creation, the core of Jacob's wands referred to the power from G-d's original creation. This is very different from a wand in the world of Harry Potter having a core from a magical animal like a phoenix or a unicorn, but it similarly connects the wand's core with its magical, or creative, source.[195]

Moses's staff (in examples two through six) is also related by the sages to the week of creation.

---

[193] As an aside, the Baal Shem Tov notes that in the Hebrew phrase for Ex Nihilo creation, Yesh Mi'Ayin, the word "yesh" that refers to created matter (literally translated as "there is") is an acronym for "right, left" (Yamin, Smol). Chassidic wordplay of this sort is beyond the scope of this book, but it further illustrates the connection between Ex Nihilo creation and the creation of the first physical dimension.

[194] Chagiga 12b

[195] The Baal Shem Tov also finds other mystical significance in the white wood of Jacob's wands, noting that the Hebrew word for white, "levena," is an acronym for the "32 paths of wisdom," the 32 heavenly paths that can be traversed in meditation, as discussed in Sefer Yetzira.

The Mishna[196] lists the staff among the special things that G-d created at twilight on the Friday of creation, just before the first Sabbath. Commentaries explain that the things listed were all things that were outside of the normal course of nature, and had to be created for a special purpose, right before G-d stopped creating and rested, starting the natural process of nature.

In example ten, the mouth of the donkey that spoke to Bilam is also listed in the Mishna as having been created at twilight of the Friday of creation.

Interestingly, none of the examples we have seen indicate that the staffs, rods, or wands in the Torah were pointed at a person or thing being magically affected. Indeed, the symbolism of the Baal Shem Tov would be clearest if the wand was held in a side-to-side direction, fitting his statement that the first dimension created was right-to-left. While there do not seem to be midrashic descriptions that include this much detail, we can certainly picture Moses, Aaron, or Joshua holding their staffs in the air in a side-to-side manner as they bring about plagues or lead the Jewish people to miraculous victory. Jacob's wands at the watering-place of Laban's sheep could also have been laid down side-to-side, as could Elisha's staff. This is all speculation, since the exact direction the staffs were held or placed does not seem to appear in the Midrash or commentaries, but it is certainly consistent with the Torah's accounts.

On a practical note, there is not any Jewish practice using wands, rods, or staffs in prayer or

---

[196] Pirkei Avot 5:6

service of G-d.[197]   The examples and commentaries quoted above do not discuss anything that we should do nowadays.   They do, however, teach us lessons about the true source of miracles and magic: G-d's unique and Divine power of creation.

From Jacob and Moses to Harry and Hermione, we see wands intimately connected to people doing magic, not only in the world of Harry Potter but also the world of the Torah.   In the Torah's view, however, these wands carry out not the desires of the people holding them, but actions decreed by the Almighty, and they channel power not from a magical creature but from G-d's original act of creation.

---

[197] The Lulav (Palm branch) that is used in prayers on the Sukkot holiday might reflect this, but commentaries do not appear to discuss it in these terms.

Go to the Hippogriff, thy Sluggard

VaYishlach

In the Book of Proverbs, King Solomon wrote the well-known verse traditionally translated as "Go to the ant, thy sluggard, consider her ways and be wise"[198]. (This is the well-known translation in old-style English, a more modern translation might be "Check out the ant, you bum, learn from it, you'll be smarter.") Commentaries explain that every animal, even the ant, was created with attributes that we can copy or learn from. Ants teach us that perseverance and teamwork can let us accomplish tasks much bigger than ourselves. Dogs teach us loyalty, and cats teach us cleanliness and grooming. Entire books have been written about Torah-based lessons from animals.[199]

While some of the magical creatures in Harry Potter are in fact discussed in Torah literature[200], many, such as the Hippogriff, are (to the author's knowledge) not, and presumably come from popular mythology or J. K. Rowling's imagination. So we can't claim to "'Go to the Hippogriff." But perhaps we can consider aspects of its story and become a little bit wiser.

---

[198] Proverbs 6:6

[199] In English, see several books by Rabbi Noson Slifkin; in Hebrew, see, Nishmas Col Chai by Rabbi Yechiel Michel Stern.

[200] See the chapter on Noah's Care of Magical Creatures

Hagrid introduces Harry's class to the Hippogriff in chapter 6 of Prisoner of Azkaban:

> *"It's polite, see? Yeh walk towards him, and yeh bow, and yeh wait. If he bows back, yeh're allowed to touch him. If he doesn't bow, then get away from him sharpish, 'cause those talons hurt....*
>
> *"That's it, Harry ... now bow...*
>
> *"Well done, Harry! ... I reckon he migh' let yeh ride him!"*

According to this story, dealing with a Hippogriff requires the following steps:

1. Show it respect, for example by bowing to it

2. Ask it to do things for you, like giving you a ride

3. Express thanks (feed it, as shown in the movie)

We see the same steps (le'havdil) in Jacob's prayer to G-d for help in the beginning of the Torah portion of VaYishlach. Jacob is approaching his first meeting with his brother Esav since twenty two years earlier when Esav had threatened to kill him. On hearing of Esav's approach with a large entourage, Jacob prayed:

"G-d of my father Abraham and G-d of my father Isaac, You told me to return to my land and my birthplace, and that all would be good. I am unworthy of all the kindness and truth that You've shown me, since I crossed the Jordan river with only my staff, and now I'm returning with two camps. Please save me from the hand of my brother Esav, for I am afraid of him, that he may kill us all, including mothers and children. You told me things would go well for me, and my family would increase like the sand of the seashore, too numerous to count"[201].

The commentary of Ovadia Sforno points out that this structure, praise followed by requests followed by thanks, was built into the Jewish prayer service by our sages. The central Jewish prayer, the Amida (also called the Shmoneh Esreh because it originally consisted of 18 blessings), starts with 3 paragraphs of praises of G-d:

"G-d the great, brave, awesome, highest of all, who does kindness for all, ... feeds all living things with kindness, ... upholder of those who fall, healer of the sick, ... Who is like You, master of all strengths, who is comparable to you?"

The prayer then proceeds with 14 paragraphs of requests that we ask G-d, consisting of all the types of things that we could possibly ask:

"Heal us, G-d, so that we'll be healthy, save us, so that we'll be saved....

"Bless on us, G-d, this year, and all types of its crops, in the best way, and give a blessing on the produce of the earth...."

---

[201] Gen 32:10-13

"Hear our voices, G-d, have mercy on us, and accept our prayers..."

The prayer then closes with thanks to G-d for everything He does for us:

"We are thankful to You, for You are our G-d and G-d of our fathers, for all eternity.... We thank you ... for our lives ... and for your miracles that are with us every day...."

This structure reflects the Torah's general approach to prayer. While prayer can certainly be a blunt request, or begging, or anything else that comes from the heart and soul, the ideal form of prayer is to first praise G-d, then make requests of Him, and then thank Him for things He's done.

As Maimonides says in his Laws of Prayer[202]:

"The mitzva is as follows: A person should pray every day, saying the praises of G-d, and after that, requesting and pleading for things he needs, and after that, giving thanks to G-d for all the good things that He gave him."

Maimonides bases this approach to prayer on the prayer of Moses [Moshe], when he begs G-d to allow him to enter the land of Israel:

"G-d my Lord, You've shown me Your greatness, Your strong hand, for who else in the heavens or on the earth can do the great things that You have done. Please be gracious to me, and show me the good land

---

[202] Rambam Hilchos Tefila 1:2, based on Talmud Brachot 32a

across the Jordan (the land of Israel), the good hill country and the Lebanon region"[203].

We see here that Moses structured his prayer in the same way as we discussed, first praising G-d in a manner unrelated to his requests, and only then making his request.

Wouldn't it be more natural and honest to ask for what we want first? After all, the things we need in our lives are more in the forefront of our minds than general praise of G-d! One Talmudic sage, Rav Eliezer, suggested that we should make our prayers more in line with human nature, first making our requests, which are foremost in our minds, and only then praising G-d, thereby putting our praises of G-d in a context where they will be psychologically more heartfelt[204]. But the Talmud's conclusion is that while this might be more honest, it is nonetheless more proper to praise G-d before asking for things from Him. This is how our prayerbooks are arranged to this day.

By considering the ways of Harry Potter's Hippogriff story, hopefully we can not only become wise, but have all of our prayers answered.

---

[203] Deut 3:24-25
[204] Avoda Zara 7b-8a

Creating Bodies

VaYeshev #1

One of the most fantastic and exciting scenes in the Harry Potter series is Voldemort's creation of a new body for himself in chapter 32 of Goblet of Fire:

> ' *"Bone of the father, unknowingly given, you will renew your son!"*
>
> *"... Flesh of the servant, willingly given, you will revive your master!"*
>
> *"... Blood of the enemy, forcibly taken, you will resurrect your foe!"*
>
> *... through the mist in front of him, [Harry] saw, with an icy surge of terror, the dark outline of a man, tall and skeletally thin, rising slowly from inside the cauldron....*
>
> *Voldemort had risen again.'*

Voldemort later refers to this feat as "old magic." Would you believe that the magical creation of a new body comes straight out of Jewish tradition, dating back to Abraham? Or that reports of this magic appear in Biblical times, the Talmudic era, and even in the twentieth century?

An early mention occurs in a commentary on the story of Joseph and his brothers. The Torah portion of VaYeshev describes Joseph as "bringing his father (Issac) bad reports about his brothers"[205]. What was

---

[205] Gen 37:2

118

this bad report? The Midrash gives a few different opinions, one of which[206] is that they had eaten "eiver min ha'chai," meat taken from an animal while it was still alive, which was prohibited by G-d to Noah and all of his descendants (in other words, all mankind). But the Midrash continues to say that they had done this in an obscure way that was permitted, making Joseph's reports slanderous.

How did they eat meat from a live animal in a permitted way? The most common answer is that they killed a cow properly, and then found an unborn calf fully formed inside it. Because the calf was still unborn and technically part of the mother cow, which had been killed properly, the calf meat was permitted to be eaten without any restrictions. (Note that it would still be non-kosher to Jews after the Torah was given[207] but was permitted to Joseph's brothers in the pre-Torah period.) This is the answer from a Jewish-legalistic perspective as to how this meat could have been permitted, and Joseph's reports slanderous.

But other Jewish sources[208] give another, more esoteric explanation: Joseph's brothers had created the calf themselves using the mystical secrets from a book called Sefer Yetzira, the book of creation. The mystical teachings of Sefer Yetzira date back to Abraham, our current text dates from the Talmudic era, and it contains the meditative techniques

---

[206] Midrash quoted by Rashi's commentary on 37:2
[207] Shulchan Aruch Yorah Deah 62:2
[208] Pischei Teshuva on Shulchan Aruch Yoreh Deah 62:2; Shnei Luchot HaBrit, 2nd comment in the individual Torah portion of VaYeshev

underlying creation of people or animals, as well as teleportation, mystical healing, and more.[209]

Practical study of these secrets, and certainly their use, fell into disrepute several hundred years ago, due to their misuse, and true understanding of the secrets of the book of Yetzira is effectively lost today. But we do know that the texts refer to a variety of meditations, each relating to the ten levels of heaven (in Hebrew, Sefirot), angels and astrological constellations, letters of the Hebrew alphabet, hours of the day and months of the year, and limbs and organs of the body. Commentaries discuss these meditations being used to magically heal medical problems in those limbs, or to bring new bodies to life.

The book of Yetzira also gives lengthy meditations on various combinations of letters in groups of two or three, along with various vowels to connect them. These letter combinations are called "tzirufim" in Hebrew, literally "combinations," and they are referred to in other Jewish meditations as well. Because letters and vowels are the basic elements of the Holy Tongue, their combinations are seen as the building blocks of life. Sefer Yetzira specifies letters corresponding to different parts of the body, which are used meditatively to heal or bring to life each body part. Each of these letter combinations can be meditated upon using each of the meditative steps listed above. Rabbi Aryeh Kaplan estimates that meditating on all the better

---

[209] In English, see the translation and extensive commentary by Rabbi Aryeh Kaplan, and the earlier chapter on Flamel and the Children of Ketura.

combinations described in Sefer Yetzira must have taken a minimum of seven hours[210].

Sefer Yetzira alludes to a number of different meditative techniques, many involving mental visualization and verbal mantras. These include:[211]

1. Looking: Letting the mind wander over something
2. Seeing: Concentrating visually on one thing
3. Understanding: Considering with non-verbal thought
4. Probing: Focusing deeply on one particular concept
5. Engraving: Removing extraneous thoughts
6. Carving: Expressing verbally

The final section of Sefer Yetzira describes these steps being used by Abraham to create new bodies:

"And when our father Abraham looked, saw, understood, probed, engraved, and carved, he was successful in creation, as the Torah writes, 'and the souls that they made in Haran'[212]."[213]

The usual explanation of that verse is that Abraham and Sarah had spread the knowledge of monotheism, bringing people's souls closer to G-d, not that they had actually created new people. But the Sefer Yetzira's interpretation is, if anything, even

---

[210] Sefer Yetzira, English translation and commentary by Rabbi Kaplan, on 2:5
[211] Obviously the techniques are more complex than our few-word summaries here.
[212] Gen 12:5
[213] Sefer Yetzira, 6:7 in Vilna Gaon edition, 8:5 in Saadia Gaon Edition

more consistent with the words of the Torah, and identify Abraham among the earliest mystics to create a new body.

Other uses of these secrets appear in the Talmud. Commentaries differ concerning whether these stories should be taken literally or figuratively, but they are certainly written as stories that took place, and are intended to teach lessons regardless of their historical accuracy. The Talmud[214] says as follows:

"Rabbi Chanina and Rabbi Hoshea would use the Sefer Yetzira every week before the Sabbath, creating a one-third-grown calf, and would eat it (for Shabbat dinner)."

The Talmud also relates the following story, explained here according to Rashi's commentary:

"(The sage named) Rava created a man using the secrets of letter combinations from Sefer Yetzira, and sent him to Rav Zeira with a delivery. [Rav Zeira] asked him questions, and the man wouldn't answer him, for he couldn't speak. Rav Zeira said to him, creation of my friend, return to dust!"

The created-man's inability to speak was because he did not have a G-d-given soul, as is discussed in the chapter Snakes, Speech, and Souls. This is made clear in the Sefer HaBahir, a first-century Kabbalistic text:

"We see that Rava created a man and sent him to Rav Zeira. He spoke to it, but it did not reply... From what could it have replied? From its soul. But

---

can a man have a soul to put in it? ... This is why it is written: 'You made him (mankind) a little less than G-d.'[215]"[216]

Rabbi Kaplan quotes other Kabbalistic sources that describe how a body is made, prior to bringing it to life. The process must be carried out by two or more people, not just one, who have immersed in a ritual bath (mikva) before beginning. The body is made from soil that has never been dug, mixed with pure spring water taken directly from the ground, never held in a vessel of any kind. Once the body is made, the people carry out the meditative process for the letters corresponding to each part of the body. But the entire process is only outlined in written sources, and many details are considered lost.

However it worked mechanically, this is what the commentaries are referring to when they say that Joseph's brothers created a calf using the secrets of Sefer Yetzira. Because the calf was their own creation and not natural, it was exempt from prohibitions about how it could be eaten.

Other citations of Sefer Yetzira span from the Talmudic era to modern days. The most famous, and the most recent (not including the X-Files episode), are from the city of Prague around the year 1580. According to legend, Rabbi Yehuda Loew, known as the Maharal of Prague, created a very strong magical creature in the shape of a man, called a "golem," to defend the city's Jews against antisemitic attacks.

---

[215] Psalms 8:6
[216] Sefer HaBahir 196, p. 78 in Rabbi Kaplan's English translation

Scholars note that the Maharal himself, while a prolific author, never wrote himself about having created a golem. But the folklore is remarkably consistent with the secrets of the Book of Yetzira and with mystical Torah concepts in general. Without ascribing truth to folklore in tourist books, it is interesting to note where it fits in with concepts from Sefer Yetzira and Jewish writings.

According to the folklore presented in Prague tourist books, a body is formed from clay that has never been used before, taken from a riverbank, and mixed with water taken directly from a river or stream. The process needs to be carried out by holy people, who awoke at midnight, recited Psalms until morning, and immersed in a mikva before sunrise. All of this is very close to the process described above from Rabbi Kaplan's commentary.

Other popular stories in Prague tourist books consistently report that the golem could communicate in a rudimentary fashion with the Maharal, but could not speak. This is consistent with our discussion above, that a person created with the secrets of Yetzira would not have a G-d-given soul, and thus would not be able to speak.

Tourist folklore also says that the creation of the Golem took six to eight hours, consistent with Rabbi Kaplan's estimates discussed above.

Interestingly, numerous books of actual Jewish practice discuss people or animals created with the secrets of Yetzira, not as theoretical or philosophical issues, but as questions that arose in practice. Certainly these scholars believed that the questions they were answering had ramifications in practice.

The Mishna Berura questions whether men created with the secrets of Yetzira can count in a minyan, a quorum of 10 required for group prayer[217]. In the middle of a discussion of laws applying to minyan counting,[218] the Mishna Berura says:

"Regarding a man created through Sefer Yetzira, and whether he can be included in (a minyan of) ten for holy purposes, see what is written in Teshuvos Chacham Tzvi and in the book Ikarei Dinim."

Even without checking the final decision, it is amazing that the Mishna Berurah, a practical and legalistic codification of Jewish law in use to this day, would consider this question to be relevant to daily life!

Why would we even consider counting a person created through Sefer Yetzira in a minyan? Chacham Tzvi[219] quotes the Talmudic statement that anyone who raises a child in his house is as if he gave birth to the child.[220] Based on this, the Chacham Tzvi suggests that a man made by Jews using the secrets of Sefer Yetzira might have the status of a Jew, having been brought into this world by Jews. In the Chacham Tzvi's words, "the good deeds of the righteous are their descendents."

---

[217] Shulchan Aruch Orech Chayim 55 Mishna Berurah 4

[218] The requirement of ten adult men for a minyan is based on the verse "you shall sanctify Me in the midst of the children of Israel" (Lev. 22:32). The Talmud (Brachot 21b, Megila 23b) teaches that the phrase "in the midst of" refers to a quorum of ten, based on other verses that use the same phrase (Num 16:21, Gen 42:5)

[219] Teshuvos Chacham Tzvi, chapter 93

[220] Sanhedrin 19b, based on Ruth 4:17 and other verses

But the Chacham Tzvi then rejects this speculation, based on the Talmud we quoted above, that Rav Zeira caused the created-man to "return to the dust," which Rav Zeira wouldn't have done if the created man had the status of a live human being that could be counted in a minyan.[221] Because of this Talmudic account, the Chacham Tzvi concludes that a man created through Sefer Yetzira cannot be counted in a minyan.

Another authority, Rabbi Tzadok HaCohen from Lublin, disagrees with the Chacham Tzvi's logic[222]. He says that any being created through Sefer Yetzira is created only for a specific purpose, and should be returned to dust after that purpose is fulfilled, to prevent it from getting out of control and causing damage. This, says Rabbi Tzadok, is why Rav Zera killed the created-man. However, for the time that the created-man was alive, it might still have had the status of a Jew, because it was created by Jews, as the Chacham Tzvi had speculated.

However, Rabbi Tzadok gives another reason why a man created by Sefer Yetzira should not be counted in a minyan. Even if such a golem had temporary Jewish status, it still wouldn't be obligated in Mitzvos (commandments) like a real Jewish man who is obligated to pray, because the golem wouldn't have a G-d-given Jewish soul, and wouldn't have the Divine reward and punishment for carrying out the Torah's commandments. Based on this, Rabbi

---

[221] Even if killing a golem doesn't constitute murder, since a golem isn't really part of "mankind," Rav Zeira wouldn't have killed him if he would serve the useful purpose of constituting a minyan.

[222] Kuntress Divrei Chalomos (in the back of some editions of Resisei Laila), ch 6

Tzadok also concludes that a man created by Sefer Yetzira could not be counted for a minyan, since a minyan by definition has to include people who are obligated to pray, not people who choose to pray.[223]

A number of authorities have analyzed more deeply the opinions of the Chacham Tzvi and Rabbi Tzadok, but for our purposes, it suffices to say that these authorities considered the issue to be one with practical ramifications.[224]

Another example of Sefer Yetzira creations discussed as practical Jewish law is the commentary that we started with above, that Joseph's brothers had eaten meat torn from a live animal that had been created through Sefer Yetzira. Pischei Teshuva is not a Midrashic commentary, it is a text in Jewish Law, and made this comment in explaining the laws of "ever min ha'chai," meat taken from an animal while it is alive. Amid all the other laws of forbidden and permitted meat, the Pischei Teshuva considered it appropriate to discuss meat from animals created through Sefer Yetzira.

---

[223] Rabbi Chayim Yosef David Azulai, known as the Chida, gives an opinion very similar to Rabbi Tzadok. Inclusion in a minyan, he writes, requires both obligation in the commandments and an understanding of to Whom we pray. According to the Chida both of these are lacking in a golem, who is not obligated to pray and who has no understanding of G-d (Machzik Bracha OC 55). Rabbi Tzadok, however, maintains that a golem might have understanding, and is missing only the Divine reward and punishment for carrying out the Torah that comes from having a G-d-given soul.

[224] For more on this subject in Hebrew, see Kuntres Sefer Yetzira in the back of the book Tzaar Baalei Chayim, by Rabbi Yitzchak Nachman Ashkoli from Ofakim, Israel.

As fantastic as it may seem, these Jewish law scholars appear to have considered laws regarding people and animals created with Sefer Yetzira to be real-world concerns that came up in practice.

In recent years, as practical use of mystical secrets like Sefer Yetzira fell into disrepute, true understanding of them is very rare. Some say that there is nobody alive today who truly understands them, and others say that nobody today has the purity of soul required for their use.[225]

Did the story of Voldemort's "old magic" have its roots in Sefer Yetzira? Probably not, since Wormtail's incantation does not include Hebrew letters, and Sefer Yetzira does not discuss bone, flesh, or blood. But the concept of creating live bodies is not limited to the world of Harry Potter. It is right there in the Torah!

---

[225] Shach, Yoreh Deah 179:18 (commenting on Shulchan Aruch Yoreh Deah 179:15)

Rights of Magical Creatures

VaYeshev #2

Hermione's Society for the Protection of Elf Welfare (SPEW) gets a lot of laughs starting in the 4th book:

> 'Not spew,' said Hermione impatiently, 'It's S-P-E-W. Stands for the Society for the Promotion of Elfish Welfare.'
> ...
> 'Elf enslavement goes back centuries. I can't believe no one's done anything about it before now.'
>
> 'Hermione – open your ears,' said Ron loudly, 'They like it. They LIKE being enslaved!'
>
> 'Our short-term aims ... are to secure house-elves fair wages and working conditions. ...'
> (Goblet of Fire, chapter 14)

This also raises an interesting question: What does Torah ethics say about the rights of magical creatures? Is Hermione taking a Jewish position when she argues that House Elves should be treated well and get paid?

It is hard to make judgments about house elves or other magical creatures from the stories of Harry

Potter when Halacha (Jewish law) stays focused on the real world, but one starting point is the previous chapter's (Creating Bodies) discussion of animals created using the secrets of Sefer Yetzira. We quoted a commentary[226] that Joseph's brothers ate meat that was torn from this type of magically-created animal while it was still alive, explaining that eating meat in such an inhumane way was OK for an animal created magically. We also quoted the story of Rav Zeira killing a man that was created through Sefer Yetzira, commanding him to "return to the dust," to lose his life. One might conclude from these stories that magical creatures have no rights, that we can treat them however we want, even "returning them to dust."

On the other hand, we see another magical creature later in the Torah, where G-d Himself seems to defend the animal's rights. Bilam (Baalam in English), the not-so-righteous non-Jewish prophet, is riding on a donkey, going somewhere in defiance of G-d. The Torah relates:

"G-d was angry that he (Bilam) was going, and an angel of G-d stood on the path to oppose him.... When the donkey saw G-d's angel standing on the road with a sword in his hand, the donkey went off the road into the field. Bilam hit the donkey to get it back to the road.

"G-d's angel then stood in a narrow path between vineyards, with a fence on both sides. When the donkey saw G-d's angel, it edged over to the side,

---

[226] Pischei Teshuva on Shulchan Aruch Yoreh Deah 62:2 Shnei Luchot HaBrit, 2nd comment in the individual Torah portion of VaYeshev

crushing Bilam's leg against the fence. He beat it even more.

"G-d's angel continued ahead and stood in a narrow place where there was no room on either side. When the donkey saw G-d's angel, it lay down. Bilam got even angrier, and hit it with a stick.

"G-d then enabled the donkey to speak, and it said to Bilam, 'What have I done to you that you hit me three times?' 'You've been tricking me!' said Bilam, 'If I had a sword, I'd kill you!'

"The donkey replied, 'Aren't I the donkey you've been riding for a long time? Have I ever done this before?'

"G-d then opened up Bilam's eyes, and he saw the angel.... G-d's angel said to him 'Why did you beat your donkey? ... If it hadn't stopped just now, I would have killed you and spared it.' "[227]

So here we see Bilam taken to task, chastised directly by an angel of G-d, for hitting his magical (talking) donkey! Why can Joseph's brother tear meat from a magical calf while it is still alive, but Bilam can't hit a magical donkey with a stick?

In general, the Torah does not speak in terms of rights, but rather in terms of responsibilities. For example, the Torah does not discuss a person's right to fair treatment, but rather the responsibility of others to treat everyone fairly, and the prohibition of treating others unfairly. In the case of animals, the discussion is not of rights of animals, but rather the

---

[227] Num 22:22-33

responsibility of people to treat animals well, and the prohibition of causing animals pain. This prohibition is called "tzar ba'alei chayim," literally "pain (or distress) to animals."

In fact, the story of Bilam hitting his donkey is one of the sources in the Torah for the halachic prohibition of tzar ba'alei chayim. Rambam[228] writes that this verse, G-d's angel asking Bilam "why did you hit your donkey," is the source of a Torah prohibition of harming animals. The Chazon Ish is quoted[229] as saying the same.[230]

So why were the brothers permitted to eat the magical animal in such a harmful way, and why was Rav Zeira permitted to kill his friend's creature?

The answer comes from considering the prohibition of tzar ba'alei chayim in more depth. Is it prohibited to bridle a horse, put a yoke on an ox, or train a dog by hitting it? The answer is no, these are not prohibited, because things that are for the animal's own good, or which are part of the animal fulfilling its constructive purpose, are not considered causing pain. Unnecessary pain that is not in the

---

[228] Guide to the Perplexed 3:17

[229] Maaseh Ish section 5

[230] As an aside, there is a long debate in the Talmud (Baba Metzia 32) about whether the prohibition of Tzar Baalei Chayim is a Torah law or a Rabbinic law. The argument centers on other Torah verses, such as the commandment to help an animal struggling under a heavy burden (Deut 22:4). Rabbi Yaakov Kamenetsky explains that the debate in the Talmud was over the obligation to reduce an animals pain, but that there is no question that the Torah prohibits directly causing an animal pain, based on the verse in the Bilam story above (Kol Yaakov (English and Hebrew) Parshas Balak; quoted in Tzar Baalei Chayim, p48 note 89).

animal's best interests and is not part of an animal's constructive purpose is prohibited.[231]

For animals created through Sefer Yetzira, it is therefore permitted to do anything to those animals that is part of the purpose of their creation. This is why Joseph's brothers could eat their magically created animal in such an inhumane way. Also, animals created through Sefer Yetzira should be destroyed after they have fulfilled their intended purpose, which is why Rav Zeira could kill the Golem after it had delivered the message.

However, Bilam was wrong to hit the donkey because it was unnecessary, causing pain due to his own anger, not the welfare or role of the donkey. In fact, Bilam was hitting the donkey precisely because the donkey was doing its job, listening to G-d's angel and taking Bilam where G-d wanted him to be taken.

We can conclude that the welfare of magical animals is important, but that each animal's welfare must be considered carefully given their natures. In the world of Harry Potter, it may be arguable that Mr. Crouch shouldn't have ordered Winky to stay in a dangerous place, but in general, if a house-elf's role is to do whatever it is told to do in service of its owners, then this servitude would not be considered Tzar Baalei Chayim, and would be permitted.

As Hagrid said in Goblet of Fire (chapter 16), about freeing house elves from their servitude:

---

[231] See Kuntres Sefer Yetzira in the back of the book Tzar Baalei Chayim for a more in-depth analysis.

"It'd be doin' 'em an unkindness, Hermione. It's in their nature ter look after humans, that's what they like, see? Yeh'd be makin' 'em unhappy ter take away their work, an' insultin' 'em if yeh tried ter pay 'em."

It seems unlikely that J.K. Rowling based Hagrid's opinion on the Torah, but they do seem similar. Magical creatures and their rights aren't just the subject of Hermione's fetish or J.K. Rowling's imagination, they are part of the Torah's view on Tzar Baalei Chayim, the prohibition of causing pain to animals.

Dreams: Divination or Digestion?

Miketz

Dreams play a central theme in several of the Harry Potter books, particularly Goblet of Fire and Order of the Phoenix, in which the magical bond between Harry and Voldemort turns Harry's dreams into a channel for seeing Voldemort's actions and feelings.

Harry, of course, knows that his dreams are far from usual. *"They're not normal dreams!"* he screams to his disbelieving friends in The Order of the Phoenix (chapter 32). He seems to know instinctively that most dreams are "only dreams," while his dreams are something more.

The Torah portions of Vayeshev, Miketz, and Vayigash also have dreams as a central theme. In Parshas Vayeshev we saw Joseph (Yosef) sold into slavery by his brothers because they did not like his dreams that prophesized Joseph's ruling over them. Now, in Miketz, we see Joseph interpreting similarly-prophetic dreams for Pharaoh, predicting seven years of financial bounty followed by seven years of famine. Joseph is then taken out of prison to help Pharaoh deal with the prophesized events.

We also see Joseph's brothers arriving in Egypt, as the famine foretold by Pharaoh's dreams becomes the springboard for Joseph's ruling over his brothers, as foretold in Joseph's original dreams. In next week's parsha, Vayigash, we see Joseph's and Pharaoh's dreams merge and come true in their entirety, fulfilling Joseph's destiny and beginning the next phase of the Jewish people in Egypt.

This focus on dreams raises an obvious question: What does Judaism say about dreams that people have in our times? Do we say, based on these Torah portions, that dreams are messages from G-d that we should interpret for hidden meaning? Or were Joseph's and Pharaoh's dreams special, and our dreams "just dreams?"

The Talmud[232] makes a tremendous statement: nowadays, when there is no prophecy, G-d sends messages to the Jewish people via dreams. In other words, dreams are to some extent the modern equivalent of prophecy. The Talmud elsewhere[233] elaborates that a dream is one sixtieth of prophesy, and that during sleep one sixtieth of our souls are returned to heaven. In other words, during sleep our souls are partly up in heaven, where they see glimpses of Divine messages.

A mystical characterization of this is given by the Zohar, the classic book of Jewish mysticism[234]:

"When a person goes to bed, his soul leaves him and rises up, ... and only a small imprint remains with the body.... When the soul leaves, it requests permission to rise...and it is told things that will happen in the near future."

---

[232] Chagiga 5b

[233] Brachot 57b

[234] Zohar Lech Lecha 83a, quoted in Chok Le'Yisroel Lech Lecha for Wednesday

This is a pretty vivid picture of the truth of dreams!

However, other comments in the Talmud seem to contradict this. For example, the Talmud[235] says that dreams "do not go up and do not come down" (in Aramaic: "eino ma'alin v'eino moridin"), that is, that they do not in any way connect between the world and the heavens. The Talmud also says that all dreams, even those that contain some truth, also contain irrelevent things as well[236]. These comments clearly contradict the Talmud quoted above, giving a belief that dreams are "only dreams."

We might think that this contradiction is just a disagreement among two different Talmudic sages, except that each side is applied as practical halacha (Jewish law) by the Shulchan Aruch. Since a single book of Jewish law, and a single scholar, applies both opinions, they must in some way be consistent.

To understand this, consider the two legal cases themselves:

The Shulchan Aruch[237] quotes the following scenario from the Talmud[238]: What happens if someone has a dream in which he swears to do something or not to do something? Is he obligated by the Torah to keep the oath, as he would be if he'd sworn while awake, or do we say that it was "just a dream?" The conclusion is that the vow is binding, and requires the legal process of nullification of

---

[235] Sanhedrin 30a, also Midrash Tanchuma
[236] Brachot 55a
[237] Shulchan Aruch Yoreh Deah 334:35
[238] Nedarim 8a

vows if it cannot be kept, implying that dreams have a portion of truth.

On the other hand, the Shulchan Aruch elsewhere[239] quotes a different scenario from the Talmud[240] with a different conclusion: A man had a dream in which his dead father appeared to him and told him where an amount of money was hidden. The money belonged to another person, who had deposited it with the father. After the son awoke from the dream, he checked in that place and in fact found money hidden there. The Talmud's question is whether he's obligated to return it to the other person, believing that it was deposited with the father as described in the dream, or whether he can keep the money as something he found. The conclusion that the son can keep the money, because "dreams do not go up and do not come down," that is, they are not assumed to be true in this kind of case. Even the dream's accuracy about the location of the money and the amount of money is not enough to give the dream a presumption of truth, since the dream may be partly true and partly untrue[241].

How can we reconcile these seemingly contradictory legal conclusions in the Shulchan Aruch and Talmud? Are dreams believed or not?

Rabbi Naftali Tzvi Yeuda Berlin, known by the acronym of his initials Netziv, gives an interesting, somewhat legalistic answer[242]. He says that dreams raise the possibility that something is true, but do not

---

[239] Shulchan Aruch Choshen Mishpat 255:9
[240] Sanhedrin 30a
[241] Encyclopedia Talmudit vol 7 p86
[242] Emek She'ela on She'iltos Rav Achai Gaon, Miketz 29, note 15

prove it. In the case of an oath, the mere possibility that the dreamer may have made a valid oath is enough to require that it be carried out or nullified, because of how seriously the Torah considers vows. In the case of a monetary dispute between two people, however, the uncertain possibility that the money may belong to someone else, based only on a dream, is not enough to require that the money be repaid. Since "possession is nine tenths of the law," a court needs definite information (not only a possibility) to force one person to pay another person.

The book Teshuvos Tashbetz[243] gives a somewhat different answer. Dreams, he says, fall into two categories. Some are prophesy-like, and the others are meaningless. The prophesy-like dreams are one sixtieth of prophesy, the meaningless ones "do not go up and do not go down." The first come from a healthy self-conscience, the second come either from an unhealthy self-conscience or, says the Tashbetz, from indigestion!

Don Isaac Abarbanel, the Spanish sage, elaborates on this idea[244]. Most dreams have a feeling of unreality and strangeness. These are the dreams that "do not go up and do not go down," whose substance comes from our imagination and not from any Divine source. In the Abarbanel's words, these dreams "are caused by food or wine, the events of the year, the mood of the dreamer or his health or sickness." Other dreams, however, feel lucid and clear, in his words, they are "completely straight, clean, without imaginary things mixed into them."

---

[243] Teshuvos Tashbetz vol 2 ch 128
[244] Abarbanel Al Ha'Torah Miketz 41

These, he says, are more often the dreams that result from our soul's freedom from the senses and its ascent to heaven, that are one sixtieth of prophecy, in some way a message from the Almighty.

A mystical perspective on this dichotomy between two types of dreams is discussed in the continuation of the Zohar quoted above:

"When a person goes to bed, his soul leaves him and rises up, ... and only a small imprint remains with the body....

"When the soul leaves, it requests permission to rise. There are many levels to rise through, occupied by husks of the light of impurity. If the soul is pure, and did not profane itself during the day, it rises [through the husks of impurity]. But if it is not pure, it profanes itself [among the husks of impurity] and sticks to them, and does not rise further.

"[When the soul rises to heaven,] it is told things that will happen in the near future. ...

"This process continues through the night, until the person wakes up and the soul returns to its place.

"Lucky are the righteous, to have G-d show them His secrets in a dream, to save them from judgment."

Understanding the mystical concepts such as souls, husks, and levels of heaven, requires more background than this book can provide, but even without full understanding we can see a consistency between the legal perspective above and the mystical perspective here.

As an aside, the idea that our souls leave our bodies in some sense when we're sleeping, even on nights where our dreams are not prophecy-like, is also reflected in the first prayer said in the morning after waking up, called Modeh Ani: "I thank You, living and eternal King, for you have returned my soul to me, with compassion and with complete reliability!"

Overall, we see a clear but multi-faceted Torah perspective on dreams: They are sometimes Divine messages that our soul receives in heaven, and they are sometimes meaningless. Unfortunately, for any one dream, there is no clear answer about whether it is prophesy or indigestion!

Returning to the Torah portion of Miketz, the Netziv asks an additional interesting question: If Pharaoh's dreams were in fact prophetic, and if Pharaoh's sorcerers were sometimes able to interpret Pharaoh's dreams, why could Pharaoh's dreams this time be interpreted only by Joseph?

He answers that sorcerers learn their knowledge from demons, and know only those secrets that demons know.[245] The Talmud says[246] that demons only know secrets that G-d announces in heaven, "behind the curtain," but not secrets that G-d only reveals prophetically to a single person. G-d's plans for Egypt had not been announced behind the curtain, but were revealed only to Pharaoh and to

---

[245] A full discussion of a Jewish perspective on angels and demons is beyond our scope here, but one approach is that G-d created demons to carry out His negative actions in the world. The idea that demons act against G-d, against His interests and out of His control, is not a Jewish concept.

[246] Chagiga 16a

Joseph[247]. The idea of demons, ghosts, and certain people hearing things from "behind the curtain" is discussed more in the chapter entitled Ghosts and Curtains.

The Torah never discusses dreams like Harry's, but the Torah perspective on dreams in general sounds remarkably similar to Harry's observation, that most dreams are perfectly natural and ordinary, but some are something more, something Divinely special.

We can never be sure how to relate to particular dreams, or where our souls went while we were sleeping, but with a clear conscience and a settled stomach, the sky's the limit.

Pleasant dreams!

---

[247] Ha'amek Davar on Gen 41:25

Everything Happens for a Reason

Vayigash #1

One of the fun aspects of the Harry Potter series is how many small details are given that are later worked into the plot in an unforeseen meaningful way. This is a trend in the entire series, and in the Torah's views on life as well.

As one example, we read at the beginning of Goblet of Fire that Winky the house elf was running in the forest in a jerky fashion, *"as if an invisible force was holding her back."* Harry dismisses this as the nature of a house elf, and so do we when we read the book, but that detail is significant later, when a full picture of the scene is revealed.

Other examples abound. The argument between Arthur Weasly and Lucius Malfoy at the beginning of Chamber of Secrets is important to Harry's later understanding of what happened with Tom Riddle's diary. The beetle in Hermione's hair and the fly in the Divination window are key to the secret Hermione figures out at the end of Goblet of Fire. The Hand of Glory in Prisoner of Azkaban and the Vanishing Cabinet in Order of the Phoenix come up again in Half Blood Prince. Throughout the books the author brings in previously-unimportant details as crucial pieces of the plot.

In the Torah portion of VaYigash we read that that life is the same way. Every detail of our lives happens for a reason, and The Almighty (if not the author of our lives, then a co-author or editor) will use these details to weave the plots of our lives and of society as a whole.

Joseph (Yosef) had been sold into slavery by his own brothers, but when he sees them years later, instead of being angry, he says the following:

"Now, do not be mad at yourselves for selling me here, because I was actually sent here before you by G-d to keep [the Jewish people] alive.... after the past two years of famine, there will be 5 more years with no crops.... And The Almighty sent me here to establish the means of your survival and great eternity."[248]

As amazing as it seems, Joseph believed so totally that things happen for G-d's reasons that he wasn't mad at his brothers for selling him into slavery![249]

Many of the things that happen in our lives feel totally random, like a ball rolling downhill without any particular direction. At times like this, we should remember particularly that in G-d's eyes nothing is random, and everything will fit into a later aspect of our lives. As angry as Joseph could have been (and certainly had the right to be) for his brothers selling him to slavery, he instead focused on the ways in which G-d used their action to achieve important and significant other aims, propelling

---

[248] Gen 44:5-7

[249] See the chapters We are as Strong as we are United and Magical Protection for more on this story.

144

Joseph to greatness and providing salvation for the Jewish people.

Rabbinic commentaries point out[250] that we see this point in the story of Joseph's sale into slavery and his life in Egypt, in the previous portion of VaYeshev. Almost every verse in the story of the parsha (3rd verse and on) starts with "and then...," the letter vav in Hebrew. The entire Torah portion is one sentence leading to another, one event "and then" another "and then" another. And that is how it must have felt at the time, events leading one to the other without any deliberation or reason. And yet we know that these events did have a Divine purpose, as we quoted Joseph saying: "I was actually sent here before you by G-d to to keep (the Jewish people) alive...."

There are exactly eight verses in the story of Joseph's being sold that do NOT start with "and"[251]. The number eight always represents the ability of the Jewish people to rise above the natural course of events, to transcend nature. The eight days of Chanukah, the eight days before a Bris, and many other Biblical events described as "happening on the eighth day," all represent the ability to transcend nature, to rise above the seven days of creation, to infuse G-d into what would otherwise be random events leading one to the other.

Rabbi Gifter, long-time Rosh Yeshiva (dean) of Telz Yeshiva in Cleveland, Ohio, added another layer to this idea. Sometimes we are able to see and

---

[250] Rabbi Frand , citing the books Shemen HaTov and Sefer HaPardes

[251] Gen 37:2, Gen 37:27, Gen 39:9, Gen 39:23, Gen 40:13, Gen 40:14, Gen 40:15, Gen 40:19

understand the reasons that something happened, as Joseph explained to his brothers. But, Rav Gifter says, there are often additional, even greater reasons for which things happen. Joseph said that he was sold into slavery to save his family from the famine, but did not relate yet the fact that the whole saga was a preparation for the Jews to be enslaved in Egypt. Likewise, the reasons that we may understand for things occurring in our own lives aren't always the end to the story; G-d's plans are often longer-term and more complex than we think.

We see this same concept, that things hapen for Divine reasons, in the story of Purim in the Book of Esther. When Mordechai was trying to convince Queen Esther to intercede with the king on the Jews' behalf, he did not appeal to her caring for the lives of her people, but rather said that the sequence of events that led to her being Queen had been Divinely orchestrated to give her this opportunity: "If you keep quiet in a time like this, salvation for the Jews will come from someone else, but you and your family will perish. Who knows if it was just for this purpose that you were put in this position?"[252]

The idea that the purpose of a series of events may only be clear at the end is referred to in Torah literature by a phrase found in the Lecha Dodi prayer sung in the Friday night prayers. The phrase in Hebrew is "sof ma'aseh, be'machshava techila," which is translated literally in English as "the last event, but the first in thought." The reason for an entire series of events, the first Divine thought that led to all the events, may only be clear from the final event that happens.

---

[252] Esther 4:13-14

These ideas give us a whole new way to think about the seemingly random events in our lives. If something significant happens, think about and appreciate all the smaller and seemingly insignificant events that led up to it. And when things happen that seem senseless, be on the lookout for major events that will tie them all together.

And of course, we're all looking forward to seeing how small details in the Harry Potter books until now (books one through six) fit into the culmination of the series. What was the instrument in Dumbeldore's office in Order of the Phoenix that showed the two snakes, and what did Dumbeldore mean by *"Yet still divided?"* Why did Dumbeldore feel triumphant at the end of Goblet of Fire when he heard that Voldemort had used Harry's blood in creating his new body? How did Fred and George predict the strange outcome of the Quidditch World Cup in Goblet of Fire? Will we ever see Dumbeldore's brother, who's been mentioned a few times but never introduced? And will any objects we have seen before turn up in Harry's search for Horcrux's, such as Tom Riddle's medal, or one of the things in Sirius's (and his brother's) house, such as the *"heavy locket that none of them could open"* in chapter six of Order of the Phoenix?

Whatever lies ahead in the story of Harry Potter, we know that in our own lives, everything happens for a reason.

We are as Strong as we are United

VaYigash #2

At the end of Goblet of Fire, Professor Dumbeldore delivers some well-chosen words about the need for unity among students and all "wizardfolk" who oppose the evil wizard Voldemort:

> *"Every guest in this hall ... will be welcomed back here, at any time, should they wish to come. I say to you all, once again - in light of Voldemort's return, we are only as strong as we are united, as weak as we are divided.*

> *"Voldemort's gift for spreading discord and enmity is very great. We can only fight it by showing an equally strong bond of friendship and trust. Differences of habit and language are nothing at all if our aims are identical and our hearts are open." (Goblet of Fire, chapter 37)*

The next year, the sorting hat, the magical talking hat whose job it is to divide the students into the four school houses, infuses the same theme into its start-of-year song:

> *"...And now the sorting hat is here*
> *and you all know the score:*
> *I sort you into houses*
> *because that is what I'm for.*

But this year I'll go further,
listen closely to my song:
Though condemned I am to split you
still I worry that it's wrong.
...
Oh, know the peril, read the signs,
the warning history shows.
For our Hogwarts is in danger
from external deadly foes.
And we must unite inside her
or we'll crumble from within.
I have told you, I have warned you...
Let the Sorting now begin."
(Order of the Phoenix, chapter 11)

The same lesson of the importance of unity is pervasive throughout the Torah and Jewish prayer. Jewish unity is both a Torah-ordained objective and a source of Divine strength.

The Torah portion of VaYigash describes how Joseph (Yosef) reveals his identity to his brothers, who had sold him into slavery 22 years earlier. Joseph had just thrown his youngest brother Benjamin (Binyomin) in jail, in order to test how the other brothers reacted, and his brothers passed the test by offering themselves in exchange for Benjamin's release.

Joseph then calmed them with an elaborate pardon for their selling him into slavery. First, he assured them that their actions were Divinely ordained in order to save the family from the famine. Second, in case they still felt shame for what they did, he told them that "it was not you who sent me here, but the Al-mighty"[253]. Last, in case they still felt remorse for Joseph's suffering during his time in Egypt, he reminded them that he had become "a lord of all [Pharoah's] house and ruler over all the land of Egypt"[254].

While we can be impressed with Joseph's willingness to let bygones be bygones, why did he go so overboard in his forgiveness? Why not let them feel some guilt for what they did? Why not at least wait for them to apologize? After all, they sold him into slavery!

Before we answer this question, consider another hard-to-understand aspect of the story. After forgiving them, Joseph was overcome with emotion and "he fell upon his brother Benjamin's neck and wept, and Benjamin wept upon his neck"[255]. This is an understandably touching scene. But a Midrash, quoted by Rashi, explains this in a puzzling way. Rashi explains that Joseph was weeping "for the two Holy Temples that were to be in Benjamin's portion of the land of Israel and were destined to be destroyed," while Benjamin was weeping over "the Tabernacle (predecessor of the Temples) of Shiloh destined to be in Joseph's portion, which also ended in destruction." This seems like a non-sequitur. Why would the brothers' reunion elicit this response from Joseph and Benjamin, and this explanation by the Midrash and Rashi?

One explanation[256] is that Joseph and Benjamin had just seen the end of 22 years of suffering caused

---

[253] Gen 45:8
[254] Gen 45:8
[255] Gen 45:14
[256] Heard from Rabbi Avraham Alter

by baseless hatred (Hebrew: sinat chinam) between Joseph's brothers and Joseph. They knew prophetically that the hatred which had torn apart their own lives was a seed that could (and would) later tear apart the Jewish people. Therefore, they attempted to begin to rectify this baseless hatred, whose root is self-centeredness, by focusing entirely on the needs of others. The tears that they shed were particularly for the loss of the other. This concern for others and their misfortunes more than one's own loss demonstrates the selflessness which is the antithesis of baseless hatred.

This is also why Joseph was so careful to alleviate any feelings which could have continued to separate him from his brothers. Anything less would be to retain some moral standing over his brothers. Instead he wished to promote unity between himself and his brothers, to combat the hatred which had caused so much suffering. What better way, than to feel his brothers' suffering, their remorse, to the point of eliminating it completely.

In fact, Joseph's entire rise to power in Egypt came as a direct result of his caring for others. Other sources point out[257] that when Joseph was in prison in Egypt, he was only released to interpret Pharaoh's dreams because he cared enough to ask two of his fellow prisoners "Why do you look troubled today?"[258] One of these prisoners was subsequently released, heard that Pharaoh needed dreams interpreted and recommended Joseph. From these four Hebrew words of concern came his entire rise to second-in-command of Egypt.

---

[257] Rabbi Frand, citing Shemen HaTov
[258] Gen 40:6

Our sages tell us that the destruction of the Holy Temples, foreseen in the Midrash by Joseph and Benjamin, was in fact a Divine punishment for the baseless hatred that existed among the Jews at that time.[259]

In fact, Jewish folklore tells us the site of Temples in Jerusalem was chosen by the Al-mighty because an incident of abundant love and devotion between brothers that occurred on that location. The full story is given in the chapter on Magical Protection, but in short, the site of the Temples was chosen because two brothers were able, on that location, to truly put each other's feelings ahead of their own, the epitome of the kind of unity that should exist between Jews.[260] But the opposite of brotherly love, baseless hatred, would cause the Temples to be destroyed.[261]

The theme of Jewish unity is found in many of our prayers and holidays.

Every month, on the Shabbat (Sabbath) before the start of the new Jewish month, we say a special prayer called Kiddush Ha'Chodesh, sanctification of the new month. This prayer includes a paragraph of hope for the Messianic era to come soon:

"May He who performed miracles for our ancestors, and took them from (Egyptian) slavery to freedom, may he redeem us too, soon, and gather us

---

[259] Talmud Yoma 9b

[260] This story is not found in primary Midrashic sources, but is quoted heavily in modern Jewish folklore.

[261] Maharal, Netzach Yisrael chapter 4; Em HaBanim Semeicha chapter 3.

from the four corners of the earth. All Jews are friends, Amen."

This prayer is clearly connecting both the redemption from Egypt and our hope for future Divine redemption to friendship and unity between Jews.

We also see the theme of unity in one of the more puzzling symbols in the Passover Seder. Passover is probably the holiday most full of symbols -- matza for redemption coming quickly, maror (bitter herbs) for the bitterness of slavery and exile, charoset (charoses) for the cement used in the hard labor of slavery, leaning on pillows during the meal signifying our having become like royalty after getting out of Egypt, and the list goes on. Chock full o' symbols!

One of the symbols which is harder to understand is mentioned in the 4th of the 4 questions: "On all other nights we do not dip our food even once, on this night (the Seder) we dip twice." This is referring to the two things that we dip during the seder, the karpas (vegetable) in salt water and the maror (bitter herbs) in charoses.

Leaving aside the fact that we do occasionally dip our food during the year (especially the salsa or guacamole lovers among us), what is the symbolism of dipping food? Why does dipping rank up there with the symbols in the other 3 questions, matza, maror, and leaning?

Rav Matisyahu Solomon[262] quotes a number of commentaries that connect these two "dippings" to two events that happened in the Bible involving dipping. The first was when Joseph's brothers sold him into slavery, and then "dipped" his coat (the "coat of many colors") into animal's blood to make their father (Jacob) believe that Joseph had been killed[263]. The second was right before the exodus from Egypt, when the Jews were commanded to "dip" a bundle of hyssop branches into animal blood and paint it on their doorposts[264], which would prevent the plague of the first born from affecting the house, and instead would make the plague "pass over" the Jewish houses.

The point of dipping branches in blood and painting it on our doors is not that they acted like pagans. The point, Rav Solomon says, is that they were symbolically taking the same act that was done previously in hatred (when Joseph's brothers sold him and dipped his coat in blood) and doing it now in Jewish unity. The "dipping" of hatred led to the exile and slavery in Egypt, while the "dipping" in Jewish unity led to the exodus and redemption. By "dipping" and painting blood on the doorposts, they were demonstrating the removal of animosity from among the Jewish people.

This is the lesson of "dipping" during the seder. Dipping can take a perfectly good tasting vegetable and make it salty, or can take something bitter and reduce the bitterness. The same action can lead to exile or exodus. While we're remembering the exodus during the seder, we have to remember how

---

[262] Matnas Chayim al Moadim, p. 281
[263] Gen 37:31
[264] Ex 12:22

154

we became worthy of Divine redemption: by taking animosity between Jews and turning it into unity.

Chassidic commentaries see the subject of unity in another place in the Passover Hagadah as well. We say[265] "for not only one has risen up against us to destroy us," which in Hebrew can also be read allegorically as saying that "only when we are not one, others will rise up against us to destroy us."[266]

The salvation of the Jews in the Purim story was also based in part on the merit of Jewish unity. Rabbinic commentaries[267] point out that at the beginning of the book of Esther the Jews are described by Haman as lacking unity:

"Haman said to King Ahasuerus, 'There is a certain nation spread out and scattered among the people....' "[268]

Later, when Queen Esther was preparing her efforts to save her people, she asked Mordechai to help her as follows:

"Esther answered Mordechai: 'Go and gather together all the Jews of Shushan, and fast for my merit.' "[269]

Esther apparently knew that Jewish salvation comes only when the Jewish people are gathered in

---

[265] In the paragraph (song) starting "ve'hee she'amda" early in the Seder
[266] Pardes Yosef vol 3 (Kedoshim), p236b, comment "be'inyan."
[267] Heard from Rabbi Avishai David
[268] Esther 3:8
[269] Esther 4:15-16

unity. According to Rabbi Shlomo Alkebetz[270], the whole reason that we give gifts of food, Mishloach Manot (commonly called "Shalach Manos"), to each other on Purim is to foster feelings of unity and friendship.

Just as the Jewish salvation remembered on Passover and Purim depended on Jewish unity, the start of the Messianic era depends on Jewish unity. The Maharal of Prague wrote that there is a spiritual force that unifies all Jews in exile, and that through this force of unity Jews will eventually leave exile and enter the Messianic period.[271]

The concept of unity is also the secret of another puzzling symbol: the four species that are brought together and waved on the holiday of Sukkot.[272] Each of the four species represents a different type of Jew, and the waving of the four species together represents Jews of different types getting together in unity. The palm branch (Lulav) has taste but no smell, symbolizing Jews with a lot of Torah knowledge but few good deeds. The myrtle branches (Hadassim) have a good smell but no taste, symbolizing Jews with a lot of good deeds but without Torah knowledge. The Etrog fruit has both taste and smell, symbolizing Jews with both Torah knowledge and good deeds, and the willow branches have neither taste nor smell, symbolizing Jews with neither Torah knowledge nor good deeds. On the holiday all four species are waved together,

---

[270] Manos HaLevi

[271] Netzach Yisrael chapter 1, discussed at length in Em HaBanim Semeicha chapter 3

[272] Lev 23:40

symbolizing Jews of all of these types getting together as one in unity.[273]

Note that unity does not mean all acting the same. The Torah describes the Jewish people as consisting of twelve tribes, each with different characters and abilities. The goal of unity is for people to maintain their differences and yet build a unified society.

Before blowing the shofar on Rosh HaShana we read Tehilim (Psalms) chapter 47. Obviously one reason is that it mentions shofar blasts. But at the end of the paragraph we read the following: "Representatives of nations gathered, the nation of the G-d of Abraham, for the protectors of the land are G-d's, He is greatly exalted." Rav Salomon explained this[274] as referring to the Jewish people whenever we gather together. We're all different, "representatives of nations," all with different customs and practices, but when we gather together for the sake of being Jews, as "the nation of the G-d of Abraham," then we have the collective ability to be "protectors of the land," and the power and beauty of this unity leads to G-d's being "greatly exalted."

In fact, unity is not only a good ethic in itself, it is the only way that any individual Jew can fulfill the Torah in its entirety. In the portion of Ki Tisa the Torah commands each member of the Jewish people to contribute a half-shekel coin yearly to the building and maintenance of the communal Tabernacle and subsequently the Holy Temple[275]. The Torah clarifies:

---

[273] Midrash Vayikra Rabba 30:12
[274] Heard from Rav Solomon, quoting Rabbeinu Yona
[275] Ex 30:13

"A rich person shall not give more, and a poor person shall not give less, than this half a shekel; each shall give this contribution to G-d, as atonement for their souls"[276].

Many commentaries explain that this particular commandment is meant to show two things. First, all Jews have the same value to G-d. Even if some are able to give more, or do more good deeds, or are more knowledgeable, nonetheless the core value of every Jewish soul is the same. Second, every Jew needs others to be truly complete. By ourselves we're all half-coins, but when joined to others we can achieve our full values.

The previous Chassidic Rebbe of Chust elaborates on this[277]. The Torah's commandments, he writes, are such that no single Jew can do them all by himself. A Jew who is not a Cohen (priest) cannot perform the Temple service without a priest, and the priest cannot do his job without a non-priest. Some commandments are for men, some for women, neither can do them all. However, says Toldos Aharon Moshe, if we form bonds of unity with other Jews, that unity shares the credit for commandments that we do, enabling us to fulfill the entire Torah in the only way that we can, in partnership with other Jews.

It is very fitting that the Torah portion of Vayigash occurs most years just before Asara BeTevet (the tenth day of the Jewish month of Tevet). Asara BeTevet is the day that Nevuzadran, the Babylonian general, laid siege to Jerusalem prior

---

[276] Ex 30:15
[277] Toldos Aharon Moshe, parshas Ki Tisa

to the destruction of the first Temple. The siege lasted almost three years until the city walls were breached and the Temple was destroyed. This is remembered every year by a day of fasting and introspection towards self-improvement on the day of Asara BeTevet, the day of the start of the destruction that our sages say was punishment for hatred between Jews.

In 1914, the Chassidic Rebbe of Belz made the following succinct statement concerning the difficult times felt by Jews of that era: "It is of the utmost importance that the Jews love one another. One must love even the lowliest Jew as himself. One must engender unity and keep far away from anything that causes disunity. The salvation of Israel during times of trouble rests on this".[278]

Note that unity does not require agreeing with everyone. The Rebbe of Belz was not suggesting condoning the actions of "even the lowliest Jew." Rather, unity means disagreeing respectfully and treating others with love regardless of agreement or disagreement, and caring about the needs of others as we care about our own[279]. Satmar Chassidic teachings explain, based on the Talmud[280], that suspecting another Jew of wrongdoing is sometimes necessary, but nonetheless is something that we should literally cry for ever having to do.[281]

---

[278] Quoted in Em HaBanim Smecha, chapter 1, page 111 in English edition

[279] Lev 19:18

[280] Yoma 18b Mishna 1:5, Yoma 19b, also Yom Kippur Musaf service in the start of the section on the Temple service.

[281] Sifsei Kehuna Sukkos 5766 p5, by Rabbi Eliyahu Katz of Kiryat Yoel, Bnei Brak

Our goal as Jews should be to have so much unity that we become "representatives of nations, the nation of the G-d of Abraham," with all of our differences and yet complete unity of purpose.

We need, as Dumbeldore said:

> "... an equally strong bond of friendship and trust. Differences of habit and language are nothing at all if our aims are identical and our hearts are open."

Magic Shows: Kosher Fun or Idolatry?

VaYechi #1

Along with the Torah's belief that magic and mysticism exist in the world, that G-d's creation includes both physical and meta-physical, is a prohibition against using improper magic in our lives:

"You shall not allow a sorceress to live."[282]

"You shall not engage in sorcery..."[283]

"Do not go to [the magical practices of] the Ovos and Yidonim"[284]

"There may not be found among you ... one who practices divination, an astrologer, one who reads omens, a sorcerer, an animal charmer, one who inquires of the Ov or Yidoni, or one who consults the dead, for anyone who does these things is an abomination to G-d...."[285]

According to most authorities these prohibitions, like most of the Torah's laws, apply only to Jews. Non-Jews can engage on sorcery as long as it does

---

[282] Ex 22:17
[283] Lev 19:26
[284] Lev 19:31
[285] Deut 18:10-12

not involve idol-worship, which is prohibited to all mankind.

Furthermore, magic accomplished through the Jewish Kabbalistic secrets of Sefer Yetzira[286] are not prohibited[287], since Kabalistic magic brings about G-d's will[288] and serves to demonstrate G-d's power in the world[289]. Rather, what is prohibited is Jews engaging in non-Jewish magic.

One of the prohibitions quoted in practical Jewish law, ruled in the Talmud[290] and the Shulchan Aruch[291], is referred to in Hebrew as "Achizas Einayim," literally translated as "seizing the eyes," referring in general to magical illusions.

What exactly is included in this prohibition of "seizing the eyes," and what does this prohibition imply about modern magic shows? Could this mean that there is a problem with magic shows?

Some authorities have said that it includes only acts of real sorcery[292] or acts that do not change nature but that use actual sorcery to create an unnatural illusion[293]. But most authorities follow the opinion of Rambam[294] that the prohibition includes sleight of hand and other natural tricks, such as

---

[286] This is discussed in chapters Making Bodies and Rights of Magical Creatures

[287] Talmud Sanhedrin 67b, Shuchan Aruch YD 179:15

[288] Rashi on Sanhedrin 67b

[289] Shach Yoreh Deah 179:18

[290] Sanhedrin 67b

[291] Shulchan Aruch Yoreh Deah 179:15

[292] Bach Yoreh Deah 179

[293] Teshuvos Rama Yoreh Deah 179:15

[294] Sefer ha-Mitzvos prohibition 32 and Hilchos Avodas Kochavim 11:9, see also Sefer HaChinuch chap 250

making coins or balls disappear or pulling a rabbit out of a hat. In the words of one commentary:

"Even seizing the eyes, which is not through sorcery, rather the appearance of it, through speed and quick hand movements, is prohibited."[295]

Could this mean that Jewish Law prohibits modern magic shows?

According to the first opinions quoted above, which say that "seizing the eyes" only prohibits actual sorcery or actions that are unexplainable, our magic shows would be fully "kosher" fun. But according to the opinions based on Rambam, that include magical illusions, it appears (so far) that modern magic shows might be prohibited as Achizas Einayim, seizing the eyes. We'll now explore this in more depth.

The Responsa Chochmas Adam[296] prohibits the Jewish magic shows of his time in very strong language, stating that they are within the prohibition of Achizas Einayim, and anyone who performs them is violating the Torah's prohibition of sorcery. Many other European and Israeli authorities agree with this conclusion, including scholars from the previous generation[297] and modern times[298].

Note that that these authorities are prohibiting Jews from performing magic shows, but they agree

---

[295] Shach Yoreh Deah 179:17
[296] Chochmas Adam 89:6
[297] Pischei Teshuvah Yoreh Deah 179:7; Kitzur Shulchan Aruch 166:4
[298] Yabia Omer vol 5 Yoreh Deah 14; Shevet HaLevi 5:129:1

that there is no problem with Jews watching a magic show performed by a non-Jew, who is not bound by the Torah's laws[299]. Jewish magicians, however, would appear to be violating the prohibition of achizas einayim, according to these authorities.

However, if we look at earlier sources in more detail, we find something interesting. Rambam describes Achizas Einayim as follows, in a discussion of the prohibition of sorcery:

"Seizing the eyes, pretending to those looking that you're doing a magical act, but not doing one, is prohibited"[300]

Rambam seems to be tying the prohibition to the image presented to the viewers, not only to the act itself. If viewers think that the magical illusion is done through actual witchcraft or sorcery, it is prohibited, but if they know it is just a trick, it would be OK.

Rashi's commentary on the Talmud[301] similarly defines the prohibited act of "seizing the eyes" as:

"Presenting the image of doing [sorcery] but not actually doing any."

It appears from these statements that magicians might only be prohibited from pretending to perform sorcery, but might not from performing magical illusions that everyone knows are just tricks.

---

[299] Darkei Teshuvah 179:15(37), Pischei Teshuva 179:7, Yabia Omer v5 YD 14, Kitzur Shulchan Aruch 166:4

[300] Rambam Hilchos Avodas Kochavim 11:9

[301] Sanhedrin 67b

This is given as practical Jewish Law by Rabbi Moshe Shternbuch[302], a contemporary authority in Jewish Law, who writes that magic shows are permitted when it is made 100% clear to the audience that the magic tricks are only tricks, and do not involve any sorcery. He also writes that the Chazon Ish, a previous-generation scholar in Israel, was of the same opinion.

Rabbi Moshe Feinstein[303], in a letter to Rabbi Daniel Neustadt in 1984, reaches this conclusion by way of a somewhat different and novel approach[304]. After surveying earlier scholarship on the prohibition of Achizas Einayim, Rav Moshe disagrees with the notion that magic shows might be prohibited, on a very simple basis: The Torah would not prohibit a person from using natural skills for innocent activity. Someone with fast reflexes, or unusual strength, or amazing speed, cannot be prohibited from using these skills just because people are surprised or puzzled by them.

In Rav Moshe's own words:

"It is astonishing to suggest that someone who naturally can move very quickly would be prohibited from using his ability of fast movement. We see that Joseph's brothers sent Naftali to Egypt to bring a receipt of sale for the family burial site from Esav to Jacob,[305] and this was permitted. Also, Samson was permitted to use his astonishing strength, that nobody

---

[302] Teshuvos ve'Hanhagos volume 1 chapter 455

[303] known as Rav Moshe, author of the responsa Igros Moshe

[304] Igros Moshe vol 8 Y.D. 4:13, and quoted by Rabbi Neustadt in an article he wrote in 2002

[305] In the Midrashic story explained in the next paragraph

else had, that clearly must have amazed others, without any fear that other people would think he accomplished it through sorcery, and certainly without fear of its being prohibited...."

The first example he brings is from a midrashic story in the Talmud, explaining the Torah portion of VaYechi[306]. Jacob's sons had brought Jacob's body to be buried in the Land of Israel, in the Machpela cave (Ma'arat HaMachpela in Hebrew) in Hebron, which Abraham had bought for Sarah's burial and which had been the family burial place since. The Midrash tells a story in which Esav, Jacob's brother, debated Jacob's right to be buried there, claiming that it should be Esav's right as first-born to be buried there instead. In the Midrash's story, the brothers had a document that proved that Jacob had acquired all the rights of the first-born, but that document was back in Egypt. One of the brothers, Naftali, had extraordinary running abilities[307], and he ran back to Egypt for the document while the others stayed at the graveside.[308]

This Midrash demonstrates, according to Rav Moshe, that use of an unusual and puzzling natural ability is not prohibited. As another example, he mentions Samson's extraordinary strength, which he used for a variety of things, which was amazing and puzzling to those who saw it, but not prohibited.

Based on this reasoning, Rav Moshe continues:

---

[306] Talmud Sotah 13a, commenting on Gen 50:13
[307] Gen 49:21
[308] The continuation of the story is interesting but not relevant to our issue here.

"A skill that the Al-mighty gave someone, to move very quickly, cannot be considered prohibited. However, if someone lies, and tells people that he's doing tricks by sorcery, this would be prohibited.... When [tricks are] done using natural means, and this is known by everyone, it would be permitted."

This issue is very interesting not only for its conclusion, but in his use of the Midrash of the story of Jacob's burial. Regardless of whether we take this midrash as literal truth, it is definitely a story used by our sages to teach lessons, and therefore must be describing actions which reflect behavior appropriate for the Biblical characters involved.

So if you want to do some real Hogwarts-style non-Jewish witchcraft, Jewish law doesn't like the idea. But if you want some good kosher fun seeing a magic show, or a good hobby using your quick reflexes for kosher fun, magic may be just the trick.

Magical Protection

VaYechi #2

At the end of The Sorcerer's Stone we learn of the magical protection that Harry received from his mother's love, particularly from her having sacrificed her life to save his:

> "Why couldn't Quirrell touch me?" [Harry asked].
>
> [Dumbeldore answered] "Your mother died trying to save you. If there is one thing Voldemort can't understand, it is love. He didn't realize that love as powerful as your mother's leaves its own mark. Not a scar, no visible sign ... to have been loved so deeply, even though the person who loved us is gone, will give us some protection forever." (The Sorcerer's Stone, chapter 17)

This concept is described later, in the 4th book, by Voldemort himself:

> "You all know that on the night I lost my powers and my body, I tried to kill him. His mother died in the attempt to save him - and unwittingly provided him with a protection I admit I had not foreseen ... I could not touch the boy.
>
> ...

His mother left upon him the traces of her sacrifice ... this is old magic, I should have remembered it, I was foolish to overlook it ...." (Goblet of Fire, chapter 33)

We see this discussed throughout the books, how Harry has magical protection imprinted on him from his Mother's act of love and self-sacrifice.

Might anything like this "old magic" appear in the Torah?

We see an interesting analogue to this kind of magical protection at the end of the Torah portion of VaYechi. After the death of Jacob (Yaacov) the Jewish Patriarch, Joseph's brothers were afraid that Joseph would take revenge on them for their having sold him into Egyptian slavery. He comforts them by reiterating that all the events had been orchestrated by G-d to bring him to Egypt for a Divine purpose:

"You decided to do bad to me, but G-d thought of it for good, to cause the events on this very day (Hebrew: KaYom HaZeh), to keep the nation alive."[309]

What does Joseph mean by "on this very day?" The most straightforward understanding is that Joseph went to Egypt as part of a Divine plan for the entire region to be saved from the famine, and for the Jewish family to be able to relocate there.[310]

---

[309] Gen 50:19-20

[310] This is discussed more in the chapter Everything Happens for a Reason.

169

The commentary Be'er Moshe, however, presents a very interesting alternative explanation, perhaps not as a literal understanding but as an allegorical lesson. The phrase "on this very day" ("kayom hazeh") is used in only one other place in the Torah's story of Joseph and his brothers, during Joseph's temptation by the wife of his master Potifar:

"And it came to pass, on this very day (KaYom HaZeh), that he went to the house to do his work, and none of the men of the house were home, that she (Potifar's wife) grabbed him by his cloak, saying 'come with me.' And he left his cloak in her hand and escaped (Hebrew: VaYanas), running outside."[311]

What does the phrase "on this very day" of Joseph's temptation by Potifar's wife have to do with the same phrase discussing the Divine reason for Joseph's going to Egypt? Be'er Moshe explains:

"The righteous Joseph (in his reassurance to his brothers, that G-d had sent him to Egypt to keep the Jewish nation alive) wasn't referring to physical survival, for G-d had already promised (Abraham) that they would have a remnant (that would always survive). Rather he was telling them an amazing thing, that the hidden purpose for which he had been brought to Egypt first ... was to face the enormous challenge (with Potifar's wife), ... because by withstanding the temptation he established the purity of life of all the Israelites, that they could resist the impurity of Egypt."[312]

---

[311] Gen 39:11-12
[312] Be'er Moshe parshat VeYechi chapter 25

Rabbi Matisyahu Solomon[313] uses this to illustrate a fascinating principle. Anytime a person overcomes a temptation to violate a Torah commandment, and manages to act in accordance with the Torah despite the temptation, he infuses his location, the ground or area he's on, with a spiritual energy that will help others succeed in carrying out G-d's will in that location.

Joseph was sent to Egypt by G-d so that he would face a strong temptation to do something immoral, and overcome it, thereby infusing Egypt with enough spiritual energy to enable the Jews to survive 400 years of slavery with their Jewish morality intact.

In fact, the Midrash says that when the Jews left Egypt, the splitting of the sea happened in the merit of Joseph. One of the Psalms that we say in the Passover Seder and the Hallel prayer service says that "the sea saw and fled (Hebrew: VaYanos)." What did the sea see? The Midrash says that the sea saw the remains of Joseph, that the Jews were transporting for burial in Israel. Because Joseph fled (VaYanas in Hebrew) from temptation, the sea fled (VaYanos) when the Jews needed it to. Put another way, because Joseph overcame human nature, the sea defied nature itself and split. Because of the continuing merit of Joseph's moral strength, the Jews were worthy of a miracle.

This same principle explains a number of other incidents throughout the Torah. For example, in Parshas Lech Lecha, when Abraham is seeing the Land of Israel for the first time, the Torah says that

---

[313] In the booklet Avita Nifla'os Mi'Torasecha, introductory chapter

he "came to the land of Canaan (the name then for the Land of Israel)... passed into the land as far as Shechem, to the plain of Moreh"[314]. Rashi's commentary, based on a Midrash, says that the significance of Shechem, mentioned as a point on Abraham's traveling to Moreh, is that he went there not just to see it, but "to pray for the children of Jacob (Yaacov) who would later battle in Shechem." Similarly, Abraham then went and built an altar in Beit El, and Rashi[315] says that he chose the location because "he had a prophecy that in the future his descendents would fall to temptation with the sin of Achan"[316]. In each case, Abraham prayed in a specific place to give spiritual protection to his descendents who would need help in the future at that very place.[317]

We also see this concept in the famous story of Moses (Moshe) and the burning bush. Moses sees the burning bush and turns off his path to investigate. G-d then tells him to stop walking, because the area around the burning bush was too holy for him to walk on, and to take off his shoes, because the ground he's already standing on is holy[318]. What is the reason for the two levels of holiness, one in which he cannot stand and one in which he can stand but only with shoes removed? Rabbi Solomon explains that the area immediately around the bush was inherently holy, so Moses couldn't go there, and the area where Moses was standing had not

---

[314] Gen 12:6
[315] Rashi on Gen 12:8
[316] Joshua chapter 7
[317] In Beit Elokim (Sha'ar HaTefila chap 18), the Mabit discusses Abraham's having engaged in all these prayers as part of his then-new role as patriarch of the Jewish nation.
[318] Ex 3:2-5

originally been holy. But after Moses left his path to explore the burning bush, which the Midrash says he did with awareness that it was something with Divine origin, the land on which he had walked became holy as well. In other words, his religiously-inspired action infused the ground he was on with so much holiness that he had to remove his shoes.

As a final example, folklore tells us that the site of the Holy Temples in Jerusalem was selected because of acts of tremendous love and self-sacrifice between brothers that happened on that spot:[319]

There once were two brothers who lived in valleys separated by a mountain. One had a family and many children, the other was a bachelor. Once, during harvest season, the bachelor, concerned with the many children his brother needed to feed, decided that at night, under cover of darkness, he would go over the mountain and place some of his own bundles of grain in his brother's field. Meanwhile, his married brother, concerned that his bachelor brother, who had no children to care for him in his old age, would need more money for his later years, independently decided on the same course of action.

In the middle of the night, each of the brothers crossed over the mountain into the other's field, and left many bundles of grain. In the morning, when each counted his bundles, they were surprised to find their full harvest, with no bundles missing. So, the next night, they each repeated the previous night's

---

[319] This story is also discussed in the chapter "We are as strong as we are united." It does not appear in any primary Midrashic sources, but is quoted heavily in modern books of folklore.

act of kindness. This continued until one night, the brothers met on the mountaintop. Immediately, each understood the events of the past few nights. They were so overcome by the other's selfless devotion they dropped their bundles and wept on each other's shoulders.

Folklore tells us that at that moment, the Almighty designated the ground where the bundles lay, a place imbued with brotherly love, to be the site where He would manifest His love to the Jewish people via the Temples.

We see that this little-known principle, that our good deeds infuse a location with positive spiritual energy, is a common denominator in all of the stories above: Joseph in Egypt, Abraham's prayers at certain places in Israel, Moses at the burning bush, and the folklore about the location of the Temples. This same principle also can be seen in practical Jewish law.

The Shulchan Aruch[320] rules that it is preferable in general to pray in a large synagogue rather than a small one, since "a large gathering is an honor to the King." The exception[321] is that when the choice is between a small synagogue in which a lot of Torah study and good deeds are done throughout the day, and a large synagogue used only for prayer, the smaller one is preferable. Why? Is not the larger crowd still an honor to the King? Rabbi Solomon explains that the influence of the spiritual energy from the study and good deeds done in the smaller

---

[320] Shulchan Aruch Orach Chayim 90:18
[321] Mishna Berurah 90:55

synagogue will help our prayers, and this outweighs the larger size crowd of the other.

The Shulchan Aruch also rules on the value of a person's establishing a "makom kavu'ah le'tefilato," a designated place to pray[322]. While doing so has many benefits, such as improved concentration, the primary reason given is that a person's regular prayer will give spiritual power to the location, which will improve the power of future prayers there.

From all of these sources we see a tremendous but little-known Torah principle, that the mitzvot (good deeds) that we do have a tangible effect on our surroundings that will give spiritual energy and protection to other people in those surroundings.

Could this kind of spiritual energy attach to a boy's skin instead of the ground in a particular place? Jewish sources do not seem to discuss it. Is this the "old magic" that protected Harry Potter, that Voldemort did not foresee? Even J.K. Rowling may not know. But if we pay attention to our surroundings, and to the mitzvot that have occurred there in the past, we may feel some of this spiritual energy in our daily lives.

---

[322] Shulchan Aruch Orech Chayim 90:19

Epilogue

There is no end to the number of Torah sources, be they stories, laws, or lessons, which can be related to Harry Potter. This book has tried to collect those that would be particularly fun, interesting, unexpected, and thought-provoking. Interested readers are encouraged to explore others, such as:

1. Giants (Order of the Phoenix): Gen 6:4 with commentary of Rashi, Sifsei Chachamim, Ibn Ezra; Num 13:32-33

2. People being magically hung in the air (Half-Blood Prince): Talmud Sanhedrin 95a, explaining Samuel 2:21:16-17

3. Killing people through speech (Goblet of Fire, also throughout the series): Rashi and Ramban on Ex 2:14; Rabbeinu Bechaya on Ex 2:12, Midrash Shmot Raba 1:34

4. Binding Magical Contracts and Unbreakable Vows (Goblet of Fire, Half-Blood Prince): Gen 24:2-3; Ex 20:7; Lev 19:12

5. Talking books (Chamber of Secrets): Talmud Megila 15b based on Esther 6:1

The same can be done for any area of life. The Torah has a lot to say about any area of interest, from world events to astronomy, from psychology to business, from calculus to food and diet.

The primary strength of this book comes from its roots in classical Torah literature. A book titled "My Own Religious Thoughts on Harry Potter" might be interesting to the "me" who wrote it, but connections to Torah sources tap into the vast web of inter-related ideas, laws, and stories, some familiar and some new, which touch our heritage and touch our souls.

Readers interested in further chapters, other related writings, and paths for exploration, can start with the book's web site at http://www.harrypottertorah.com

Sources quoted

Abarbanel, Don Isaac: Spanish sage and author, lived 1437-1508. Finance Minister for the Spanish government of King Ferdinand and Queen Isabella immediately before the Spanish expulsion. (Dreams)

Alkebetz, Rav Shlomo: Scholar and mystic in the town of Tzefat (Safed), author of the Lecha Dodi prayer sung on Friday nights. (Unity)

Alter, Rav Avrohom Mordechai: Contemporary scholar and Jewish outreach professional in Chicago, IL. (Unity)

Amudei Kesef: Analytic and Halachic work by Rabbi Shabsai ben Eliezer Zusman Katz, first published 1883 in Warsaw, reprinted 1990. Currently out of print, but quoted in Pischei Teshuva and other sources. (Day of Magic)

Ashkoli, Rav Yitzchak Nachman: see Tzaar Baalei Chayim (Creating Bodies, Rights of Magical Creatures)

Azulai, Rabbi Chayim Yosef David: Known as the Chida, the initials of his name, lived in Jerusalem and Italy, 1724-1806. Author of Machzik Bracha on Jewish law, and many other works of Jewish law and mysticism. (Creating bodies)

Baal Shem Tov: Founder of the Chassidic movement, lived roughly 1700-1760. (Magic Wands)

Bach: Bayit Chadash, one of the classic commentaries on the Tur, the predecessor to the Shulchan Aruch in

Ashkenazi Halachic writings. Written by Rabbi Yoel Sirkis, 1561-1640. (Magic Shows)

Bahir: One of the classical mystical texts, written in the times of the Mishna, attributed to Rabbi Nechunia ben HaKana. One of the most influential Kabbalistic texts, quoted often in Ramban's commentary on the Torah, and paraphrased often in the Zohar. (Creating Bodies)

Be'er Moshe: Moral lessons from the weekly Torah portions, written by Rabbi Moshe Yechiel Epstein, the Rebbe of Ozhrov, lived 1889-1971 in Ozhrov, New York, and Israel. (Magical protection)

Bechaya, Rabbeinu: The Torah commentary of Rabbeinu Bechaya ben Asher, written in Spain in 1291. (Snakes, epilogue)

Beit Elokim: See Trani (Magical protection)

Belzer Rebbe: Rebbe of the Chassidic dynasty of Belz before and during the Holocaust. (Unity)

Berlin, Rabbi Naftali Tzvi Yehuda: Also known as "the Netziv" from the initials of his Hebrew name. Lived 1817-1893. Author of Ha'amek Davar (sometimes called Emek Davar), Emek She'ela, and other commentaries. (Owl Post, Ghosts, Dreams, Magic Wands)

Be'Simcha u've'Tov Levav: Contemporary book (in Hebrew) on the subject of happiness and enjoyment in Jewish thought, by Rav Hadar Yehuda Margolin of Jerusalem, Israel. (Everyday Magic)

Biyur Halacha: By the author of the Mishna Berurah, and published alongside it, giving more in-depth analysis of some of its rulings. (Magic Words)

Blazer, Rav Yitzchak: See Ohr Yisroel

179

Breslov, Rav Nachman: Founding Rebbe of the Breslover Chassidic dynasty. Lived 1772-1810. (Wands)

Chacham Tzvi: By Rabbi Tzvi Hirsh Ashkenazi (1660-1718), applying Jewish Law to then-modern questions. (Creating Bodies)

Chatam Sofer: Rabbi Moshe Sofer, scholar, expert on Jewish Law, lived 1762-1838. Author of commentaries and answers to practical questions in Jewish practice. (Day of Magic)

Chazon Ish: Primary set of books on Jewish Law by Rabbi Avraham Yeshaya Karelitz (lived 1878-1953), applying Jewish Law to contemporary issues. (Animal Rights, Magic Shows)

Chida: See Azulai.

Chochmas Adam: Commentary by Rabbi Avraham Danzig, 1748-1820, on areas of Jewish Law relating to the Yoreh Deah section of the Shulchan Aruch. (Magic Shows)

Chok LeYisrael: Book designed for daily study, written in the 1500's by students of the AriZal in Tsfat (Safed), to enable learning of all areas of Torah in spare time. Consists of Torah, Prophets, Writings, Mishna, Gemorah, Halacha, Mussar (character development), and Kabbalah. (Magic Words, Abraham's Tree, Dreams)

Chuster Rebbe: Contemporary Chassidic Rabbi, orginally from America, currently living in Beit Shemesh, Israel. The current Chuster Rebbe published the book Toldos Aharon Moshe, written by his father the previous Chuster Rebbe. (Ghosts, Unity)

Daas Zekeinim: Torah commentary from the Tosfos school of Talmudic analysts, from 12-14th century France. (Flamel)

Darkei Teshuvah: Halachic Commentary on the Yoreh Deah section of the Shulchan Aruch, written in 1893, by Rabbi Tzvi Hirsch Shapira, a Chassidic leader in Hungary. (Magic shows)

David, Rabbi Avishai: Contemporary scholar, Rabbi, and educator, currently living in Beit Shemesh, Israel. (Unity)

Diskin, Maharil: Commentary on the Midrash by Rabbi Yehuda Leib Diskin (1818-1898). (Noah's Magical Creatures)

Divrei Yoel: See Satmar Rebbe

Em HaBanim Semeicha: By Rabbi Yissocher Dov Teichtal (1885-1945), a compendium of hundreds of sources, supporting the author's original thoughts, on the importance of the Land of Israel and Jewish unity, especially in light of the holocaust. (Everyday Magic, Day of Magic, Unity, Magic Wands)

Emek She'ela: See Berlin

Encyclopedia Talmudit: Contemporary encyclopedia of Talmudic concepts and issues. (Dreams)

Feinstein, Rav Moshe: Halachic authority in pre-war Europe and post-war America, lived 1895-1986. Forerunner in applying Jewish law to modern circumstances. His responses to questions are collected in Igros Moshe (in Hebrew) among other books. (Magic shows)

Frand, Rabbi Yissochar: Contemporary scholar and English-language speaker and author, currently living in Baltimore, Maryland. (Mudbloods, Happens for a Reason, Unity)

Gifter, Rav Mordechai: Post-holocaust Rosh Yeshiva of Telz (Telshe) Yeshiva, in Cleveland, Ohio. (Happens for a reason)

Guide to the Perplexed: See Rambam

Gur Aryeh: See Maharal (Flamel)

Ha'amek Davar: See Berlin, Rav Naftali Tzvi

Haber, Rabbi Yaacov: Contemporary scholar, educator, and outreach professional. Formerly Director of Jewish Education for the Orthodox Union, now founder of TorahLab. Rabbi in Buffalo, NY, Melbourne, Australia, Monsey, NY, and Jerusalem. (Day of Magic)

Ha'Ksav ve'ha'Kabbalah: Torah commentary written in 1839 by Rabbi Yaakov Tzvi Meklensburg, combining mysticism with linguistic analysis. (Magic Wands)

Ibn Ezra: Scholar, grammarian, astronomer, philosopher, and author of a Torah commentary and other works. Lived in Spain, 1089-1167. (Snakes, Magic Wands)

Igros Moshe: See Feinstein

Kamenetsky, Rav Yaakov: Contemporary Rabbi, Rosh Yeshiva (dean) of Yeshiva Torah Va'daas in New York until his death in 1986 at the age of 95. Author of the Kol Yaakov Torah commentary, among other works. (Rights of Magical Creatures)

Kaplan, Rabbi Aryeh: Contemporary English author until his death in 1983. Worked as a physicist until devoting himself to Jewish writings. He revealed to the modern ready many concepts previously known only by scholars, particularly mystical concepts. (Ghosts, Flamel, Creating Bodies)

Katz, Rabbi Eliyahu: See Sifsei Kahuna

Kitzur Shulchan Aruch: Written by Rabbi Shlomo Ganzfried (1804-1886) in Hungary, to reflect day-to-day Jewish law in a straightfoward fashion. (Magic shows)

Kol Yaakov: See Kamenetsky, Rabbi Yaakov

Kuntres Sefer Yetzira: See Ashkoli

Lekutei Mohoran: See Breslov

Levitansky, Rabbi Ahron: Contemporary scholar and teacher, formerly a Jewish Outreach expert in Chicago, IL, and now educator in Cleveland, OH. (Abraham's Tree, Destiny)

Leow, Rav Yehuda: See Maharal

Luzatto, Rav Moshe Chayim: Known as the Ramchal, an acronym for his name. Lived 1707-1746. (Introduction)

Maaseh Ish: See Chazon Ish (Rights of Magical Creatures)

Mabit: See Trani (Magical protection)

Machzik Bracha: See Azulai.

Maharal: Rabbi Yehuda Leow, known as the Maharal of Prague. Born in Posen in approximately 1513, died in Prague in approximately 1609. Author of numerous works, including many philosophical works, as well as the Gur Aryeh meta-commentary on Rashi's Torah commentary. Famous for "decompartmentalizing" Torah, stressing connections between Talmud and Halacha, as well as study of Kabbalah. (Magic words, Mudbloods, Creating Bodies, Flamel, Unity)

Maharasha: Classic commentary on the Talmud, focusing on explaining the Midrashic (Aggadic) portions, written in 1612 by Rabbi Shmuel Eliezer Aidel. (Snakes, Flamel, Magic Wands)

Maimonides: See Rambam

Mandelbaum, Rav Alexander Aryeh: Contemporary scholar and author (in Hebrew) living in Jerusalem. (Mudbloods, Magic Wands)

Manos HaLevi: See Alkebetz

Margolin, Rav Hadar Yehuda: See Be'Simcha u've'Tov Levav (Everyday magic)

Matnas Chayim: See Solomon

MiMa'amakim: See Mandelbaum

Mishna Berurah: Classic Jewish law text written by Rabbi Yisrael Meir Kagan (lived 1838-1933, author of Chofetz Chayim) in the 1920's, commenting on the Orech Chayim (daily life) section of the Shulchan Aruch, and elaborating on the Ashkenazic practices of the time. (Magic words, Everyday Magic, Creating Bodies)

Nachmanides: See Ramban

Nefesh HaChayim: Philosophical and mystical book by Rav Chayim of Volozin. (Magic words)

Netzach Yisrael: see Maharal

Netziv: See Berlin

Neustadt, Rabbi Daniel: Contemporary scholar, teacher, and writer (in English) on issues in practical Jewish law, currently living in Cleveland, OH. (Magic shows)

Nishmat Kol Chai, by Rabbi Yechiel Michel Stern in Jerusalem, contemporary book (in Hebrew) collecting

Torah sources relating to a wide variety of animals. (Noah's Magical Creatures, Owl Post, Hyppogriff)

Ohr Yisrael: Philosophical writings based largely on the teachings of Rav Yisroel Salanter (1810-1883), founder of the Mussar Movement focusing on ethical growth, written by his disciple Rav Yitzchak Blazer. Originally written in Hebrew in the late 1800's, it was recently translated into English by Rabbi Zvi Miller. (Ghosts)

Onkolus: Classic interpretive translation of the Torah into Aramaic, from the mishnaic era, written around 90 CE , known as "The Targum," meaning "the translation." (Magic Wands)

Pischei Teshuva: Classic commentary on the Yoreh Deah section of Shulchan Aruch, by Rabbi Avraham Tzvi Eisenstadt in 1836. (Day of Magic, Creating Bodies, Magic Shows)

Rabbeinu Yona: Scholar and author from 12th century Spain, in the town of Gerona, and author of Sha'arei Teshuva and a number of other commentaries and books. (Unity)

Rambam: Rabbi Moshe ben Maimon, a.k.a. Maimonides. Famous Egyptian expert in Jewish law and philosophy, lived 1135-1204. (Hippogriff, Rights of Magical Creatures, Magic Shows)

Ramban: Rabbi Moshe ben Nachman, a.k.a. Nachmanides. Lived 1194-1270. Commentator and mystic, author of commentaries on the Torah and Talmud, as well as a number of other books. (Owl Post, Magic Wands, epilogue)

Ramchal: See Luzatto

Rashi: Premier classic comentary on the Torah and Talmud, usually printed alongside both. Lived 1040-1105. (Quoted in almost every chapter)

Resisei Laila: See Tzodok HaCohen of Lublin

Ritva: Rabbi Yom Tov ben Avraham, lived 1248-1330, spiritual leader of Spain, and author of a Talmudic commentary, emphasizing the non-legalistic portions of the Talmud. (Ghosts)

Sa'adia Gaon: Saadia ben Yosef, leading scholar of the gaonic period, lived 882-942 CE, head of the famed Yeshiva in Pumbedisa. (Flamel)

Salanter, Rav Yisroel: See Ohr Yisroel. (Ghosts)

Satmar Rebbe: Rebbe of the Satmar Chassidic sect during and after the Holocaust. (Abraham's Tree)

Sefer HaChinuch: Anonymously-authored work on the 613 mitzvot, according to their order in the Torah, first published in 1523. (Magic Shows)

Sefer HaMitzvos: See Rambam

Sefer HaPardes: Collection of Jewish thoughts from the school of Rashi. (Happens for a reason)

Sefer Yetzira: Classic mystical text, whose tachings are attributed to Abraham (18th century BCE), and whose text was first written in the times of the Mishna in the first century of the common era. Referred to in the Talmud and early commentaries as a primary source of Kabbalistic magic. (Flamel, Creating Bodies, Rights of Magical Creatures)

Seforno, Rabbi Ovadia: Italian sage, author of (among other works) a Torah commentary first published in 1567. (Snakes, Hippogriff)

Shach: Sifsei Cohen commentary on the Shulchan Aruch, written by Rabbi Shasai Cohen (1622-1663). (Magic Shows)

She'iltos Rav Achai Gaon: The first known post-Talmudic book of Jewish Law, written around 700 CE by Rabbi Achai of the Gaonic period. (Dreams)

Shevet HaLevi: Contemporary collections of answers to modern-day questions in Jewish Law, by Rabbi Shmuel Wosner of Bnei Brak, Israel. (Magic shows)

Shemen HaTov: Torah commentary by Rabbi Dov Weinberger, a contemporary Rabbi in New York. (Happens for a reason, Unity)

Shita Mekubetzes: A collection of Talmud commentary by Rabbi Betzalel Ashkenazi, the teacher of the AriZal, explaining the opinions of the earlier generation of Talmudic commentaries. (Ghosts)

Shnei Luchot HaBrit: Esoteric commentary on the Torah by Rabbi Yeshaya Segal HaLevi Horowitz (approx 1565-1630), known as the Shla, the Hebrew initials of the book title. Initially a Rabbi in Prague, later in Jerusalem. (Creating Bodies, Rights of Magical Creatures)

Shternbuch, Rav Moshe: Contemporary authority on Jewish Law and prolific author, previously in England and South Africa and then in Jerusalem. Leading figure in the Eida Chareidis of Jerusalem. (Destiny, Magic Shows)

Shulchan Aruch: Classic text on Jewish Law written by Rav Yosef Karo in Israel in the 1500's, bringing together Jewish law opinions from earlier primary sources, incorporating Ashkenazic opinions but emphasizing Sefardic opinions. It was immediately amended with Ashkenazic opinions by Rav Moshe Isserlis, and the combined text has served as the basis of

Jewish Law since. (Magic words, Day of Magic, Creating Bodies, Dreams, Magic Shows)

Sifsei Kehuna: Contemporary booklets on holidays and other Torah thoughts, from Rav Eliyahu Katz, the Rabbi of Beit Midrash VaYoel Moshe, in the Satmar Chassidic neighborhood of Bnei Brak, Israel. (Unity)

Slifkin, Rabbi Noson: Contemporary scholar and author (in English) on the subject of animals in Torah literature, currently living in Ramat Beit Shemesh, Israel. (Noah's Magic Creatures, Hippogriff)

Solomon, Rav Matisyahu: Contemporary scholar, speaker (in English), and author (in Hebrew), formerly at the Yeshiva of Manchester, England, and currently at Bais Midrash Gavo'ah in Lakewood, NJ. (Unity, Magical protection)

Solovetchik, Rav Yosef Ber: Former Rosh HaYeshiva (Dean) of Yeshiva University, Rabbi in Boston, and leading scholar and thought leader of large segments of modern Orthodoxy in America. Lived 1903-1993. (Mudbloods)

Stern, Rabbi Yechiel Michel: See Nishmat Kol Chai

Teichtal, Rav Yissocher Dov: See Em HaBanim Semeicha

Teshuvos Rama: Questions-and-answers on Jewish Law from the 1500's, by Rav Moshe Isserlis, author of the Ashkenazic amendments to the Shulchan Aruch. (Magic Shows)

Teshuvos Tashbetz: Responsa by Rabbi Shimon Duran, written in the 15th century in Spain. (Dreams)

Teshuvos ve'Hanhagos: See Shternbuch

Toldos Aharon Moshe: See Chuster Rebbe

Torah Shleima: Encyclopedic Torah commentary by Rabbi Menachem Mendel Kasher, collecting and commenting on all references to Torah verses from the Talmudic and Midrashic era. (Abraham's Tree, Flamel, Destiny, Magic Wands)

Tosfos: Classic commentary on the Talmud, printed alongside the Talmudic text (and Rashi's commentary) in almost all printed editions of the Gemorah. (Ghosts)

Trani, Rabbi Moshe ben Yosef: Known as the Mabit, author of Beit Elokim and other far-reaching works of Jewish philosophy. Lived in Tzefat (Safed), Israel, in the 16th Century CE. (Magical protection)

Tzaar Baalei Chayim: Contemporary book (in Hebrew) on the subject of treatment of animals, by Rav Yitzchak Nachman Ashkoli, a scholar living in Ofakim, Israel. (Creating Bodies, Rights of Magical Creatures)

Tzadok HaCohen, Rabbi: Chassidic Rabbi from the town of Lublin, lived 1823-1900, author of many works, including Pri Tzaddik and Resisei Laila. (Creating Bodies)

Vilna Gaon: Rabbi Eliyahu of Vilna, lived 1720-1797, leader of non-Chassidic Jewry of the time, prolific author and master of both intellectual Torah study and Kabbalistic mysticism. (Magic Words)

Yabia Omer: Contemporary Jewish law responsa, by Rabbi Ovadia Yosef, leading Sephardic scholar in Israel. (Magic shows)

Yad Chazakah: See Rambam

Yafeh Toar: Classic commentary on Midrash Rabba, by Rabbi Shmuel Yafeh Ashkenazi. (Noah's Magical Creatures)

Yetzira: See Sefer Yetzira

Yosef, Rabbi Ovadia: See Yabia Omer.

Zohar: Classic mystical Kabbalah text, written in the Mishnaic era, around 120 CE, by Rabbi Shimon Bar Yochai. (Magic Words, Tree, Flamel, Dreams)

Index of Citations

Biblical citations

Gen 1:1 22
Gen 1:2 23
Gen 1:3 22
Gen 1:7 99
Gen 1:11 23
Gen 1:14 23
Gen 1:20 23
Gen 1:24 23
Gen 1:26 23
Gen 1:29 23
Gen 2:1-3 33
Gen 2:18 23
Gen 2:7 27
Gen 3 27
Gen 3:1 28
Gen 3:6 42
Gen 6:4 176
Gen 8:4-12 46
Gen 8:7 ....47, 49
Gen 9:15 62
Gen 12:5 ....87, 121
Gen 12:6 ....107, 172
Gen 12:8 172
Gen 14:18 4
Gen 16:6-13 82
Gen 18:3-4 70
Gen 18:4 71
Gen 19:21-23 92

Gen 19:22 95
Gen 19:31-33 61
Gen 21:33 71
Gen 24:1-15 78
Gen 24:2-3 176
Gen 24:34-45 78
Gen 24:42 78
Gen 25:5-6 86
Gen 25:6 88
Gen 27:28 93
Gen 27:39-40 94
Gen 28:10-11 79
Gen 28:15 107
Gen 28:17 79
Gen 29:16-30 97
Gen 29:17 98
Gen 30:31-43 102
Gen 30:37 107
Gen 32:10-13 115
Gen 32:11 105
Gen 32:8 91
Gen 37:2 118
Gen 37:31 154
Gen 38 63
Gen 39:11-12 170
Gen 40:6 151
Gen 41:25 .... 58, 142
Gen 42:5 125
Gen 44:5-7 144
Gen 45:14 150
Gen 45:8 150
Gen 49:21 166
Gen 50:10 54
Gen 50:13 166
Gen 50:19-20 169
Ex 2:12,14 176
Ex 3:2-5 172

Ex 4:2-5 103
Ex 7:10 106
Ex 7:17-20 103
Ex 7:9 106
Ex 7:9-13 103
Ex 8:1 103
Ex 8:12-13 103
Ex 9:23 103
Ex 10:13 103
Ex 12:22 154
Ex 14:16 103
Ex 17:5 103
Ex 17:9-12 104
Ex 20:7 176
Ex 20:8-11 33
Ex 22:17 161
Ex 30:13 157
Ex 30:15 158
Ex 35:3 34
Lev 17:11 48
Lev 19:12 176
Lev 19:18 159
Lev 19:26 161
Lev 19:26,31 36
Lev 19:31 161
Lev 23:40 156
Lev 23:42-43 72
Num 13:32-33 176
Num 16:21 125
Num 16:32 31
Num 17:20-24 104
Num 20:11 103
Num 20:8 106
Num 22:22-33 ....30, 131
Num 22:27-28 104
Num 25:7 104
Num 29:2 99

Deut 3:24-25 117
Deut 10:12 97
Deut 18:10-12 .... 36, 161
Deut 22:4 132
Deut 28:47 8
Deut 34:4 51
Joshua 7 172
Joshua 8:18, 8:26 104
Judges 13:20-25 82
Samuel 1:1:13 20
Samuel 2:21:16-17 .... 79, 176
Kings 1-17:6 49
Kings 2:4:29-31 105
Esther 3:8 155
Esther 4:13-14 146
Esther 4:14 66
Esther 4:15-16 155
Esther 6:1 176
Job 14:21 52
Job 14:22 .... 52, 54
Job 29:18 .... 40, 42
Proverbs 6:6 113
Psalms 106:30 106
Psalms 8:6 123
Psalms 89:21 62
Ruth 4:17 125

Talmudic citations

Brachot 15a 18
Brachot 15b 19
Brachot 18b 51, 52, 56
Brachot 21b 125
Brachot 32a 116
Brachot 33b 97
Brachot 55a 137

Brachot 57b 136

Shabbos 113b 22

Shabbos 152 54

Pesachim 68a..105

Rosh HaShana 29a Mishna 3:8 105

Rosh HaShana 32a 22

Yerushalmi Rosh HaShana 4:8 99

Yoma 9b 152

Yoma 18b Mishna 1:5 159

Yoma 19b..159

Sukkah 41a 38

Megila 10b 64

Megila 15b 176

Megila 21b 22

Megila 23b 125

Megila 25a..97

Chagiga 5b 136

Chagiga 12b 110

Chagiga 15a..57

Chagiga 16a..57, 141

Nedarim 8a...137

Sota 10a 71

Sota 13a..166

Sota 34b..52

Sota 49a..57

Baba Metzia 32 132

Baba Metziah 59a..56

Baba Basra 123a..98

Sanhedrin 19b 125

Sanhedrin 30a...137, 138

Sanhedrin 59b 28

Sanhedrin 65b 122

Sanhedrin 67b 162, 164

Sanhedrin 91a..86

Sanhedrin 95a...79, 176

Sanhedrin 108b 40

Avoda Zara 7b-8a..117

Pirkei Avot 5:6 111
Pirkei Avot 5:9 31
Pirkei Avot 5:25 7
Chulin 91b 79

Subject index

Acupuncture, 89

Alchemy, 85

Animals, 26, 40, 46, 113, 129

Asara BeTevet, 159

Bais HaMikdash. *See* Temple

Belz, 159

Chana, 20

Creation of the universe, 21, 33, 108

Demons, 57, 86, 141

Etrog, 156

Eve, 28, 42

Four species, 156

Garden of Eden, 27, 42

Ghosts, 50

Golem, 32, 122, 123

Haftara

  Naso, 82

  VaYeira, 105

Havdala, 73

Israel, 51, 107, 116

Korbanot. *See* Sacrifices

Lineage, 61

Lulav, 156

Minyan, 125

Moses, 51, 67, 103, 116, 172

Moshiach, 62, 152, 156

Mourning, 55

New month, 152

Palm reading, 100

Passover, 103, 153, *171*

Prayer, 19, 114, *174*

  Baruch She'amar, 22

    Lecha Dodi, 146
    Modeh Ani, 141
    New month, 152
    Shema, 18
    Yigdal, 14
Purim, 66, 146, *155*
Repentance, 99
Rosh HaShana, 53, 99, *157*
Sabbath, 22, 33, 73
Sacrifices, 99
Samson, 82, 165
Satmar, 72, 159
Sefer Yetzira, 87, 110, 119, 130, 162
Shabbat, Shabbos. *See* Sabbath
Shma, 18
Sorcery, 36, *161*
Speech, 17
Sukkot, 72, 112, 156
Tefillin, 89
Temple, 66, 150, 152, 173
Teshuva. *See* Repentance
Tisha B'Av, 57
Torah study, 20, 57, 80
Yom Kippur, 57, 100, 159

7730579R0

Made in the USA
Lexington, KY
11 December 2010